Tony Vandrulin.
from Ma...

C000228468

AA

walking in Norfolk

First published 2008

Produced by AA Publishing
© Automobile Association Developments Limited 2008

All rights reserved. No part of this publication may be reproduced, stored in a retrieval system, or transmitted in any form or by any means – electronic, photocopying, recording or otherwise – unless the written permission of the publishers has been obtained beforehand.

Published by AA Publishing (a trading name of Automobile Association Developments Limited, whose registered office is Fanum House, Basing View, Basingstoke, Hampshire RG21 4EA; registered number 1878835)

Visit the AA Publishing website at www.theAA.com/travel

This product includes mapping data licensed from Ordnance Survey® with the permission of the Controller of Her Majesty's Stationery Office.
© Crown copyright 2008. All rights reserved. Licence number 100021153

ISBN-13: 978-0-7495-5871-0

A CIP catalogue record for this book is available from the British Library.

The contents of this book are believed correct at the time of printing. Nevertheless, the publishers cannot be held responsible for any errors or omissions or for changes in the details given in this book or for the consequences of any reliance on the information it provides. This does not affect your statutory rights. We have tried to ensure accuracy in this book, but things do change and we would be grateful if readers would advise us of any inaccuracies they may encounter.

We have taken all reasonable steps to ensure that these walks are safe and achievable by walkers with a realistic level of fitness. However, all outdoor activities involve a degree of risk and the publishers accept no responsibility for any injuries caused to readers whilst following these walks. For more advice on walking safely see page 112.

Some of these routes may appear in other AA walks books.

Researched and written by Beau Riffenburgh and Liz Cruwys
Field checked and updated 2007 by Clive Tully and Tony Kelly

Managing Editor: David Popey
Layout and Design: Tracey Butler
Image Manipulation and Internal Repro: Sarah Montgomery
Series Design: Liz Baldin at Bookwork Creative Associates for AA Publishing
Cartography provided by the Mapping Services Department of AA Publishing

A03624

Repro by Keenes Group, Andover
Printed by Leo Paper Group in China

PAGES 2–3: *Golden sunset through reeds on the lakeside of Horsey Mere*
RIGHT: *Boats stranded in Harbour at low tide at Wells-next-the-Sea*
PAGES 6: *A sailboat moored at Horsey Mere*

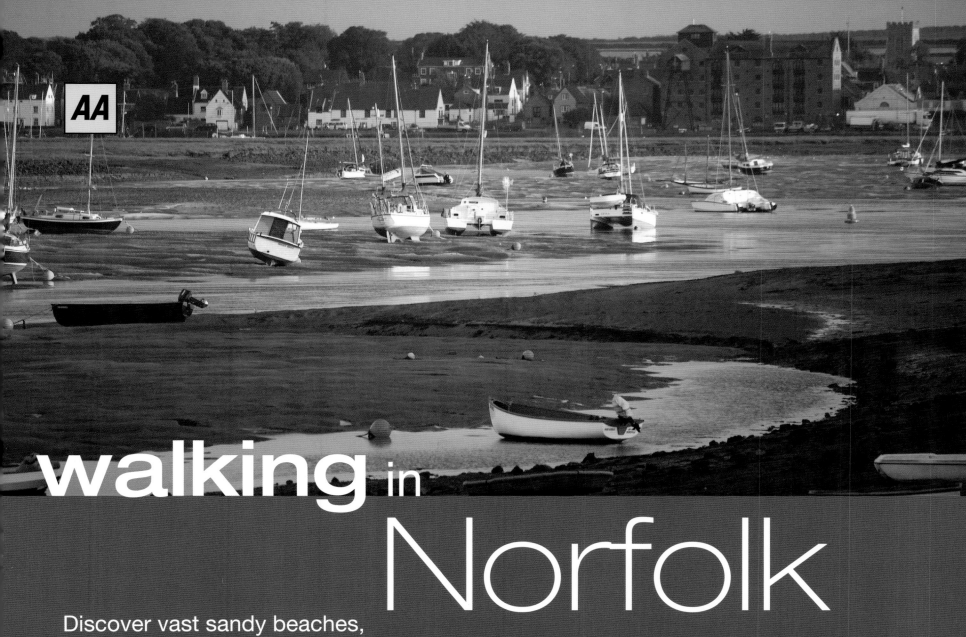

walking in Norfolk

Discover vast sandy beaches,

peaceful woodland and gently

rolling countryside

Contents

This superb selection of walks introduces the themes and characters that define the beautiful landscape of Norfolk.

Introducing Norfolk

Reed-fringed lakes, vast sandy beaches, mysterious marshland, teeming wildlife reserves and peaceful, pine-scented forests. Norfolk offers all these and more to walkers, and is one of the most varied and interesting counties in England. It boasts the gorgeous Broads, the wild and heathy Breckland, a stunning coastline and huge areas of fen and marsh. It also has more than its share of long distance footpaths, the best known of which are the Norfolk Coast and Peddars Way path, the Weavers' Way, Marriott's Way, Hereward Way and Boudica's Way.

An Extraordinary Landscape

Norfolk, and East Anglia in general, have a reputation as being flat and featureless, but the reality could not be more different. The Cromer Ridge and the gently rolling countryside to the south provide some slopes to put your legs through their paces, while you are presented with changing and diverse scenery at every turn. There's a medieval fortress at Castle Acre and splendid country houses and stately homes at Blickling, Sandringham and Holkham. There are lonely ruined priories, to remind you of the power the Church once held in this populous county, and plenty of strongholds raised by the Romans to repel Saxon invasions – see Burgh Castle near Great Yarmouth and Caister St Edmunds near Norwich. There are pleasure parks on the coast, a bird sanctuary at Horsey Mere, and farms that fill the air with the sweet scent of lavender, roses and herbs. There are also museums, art galleries and theatres. In short, Norfolk has it all!

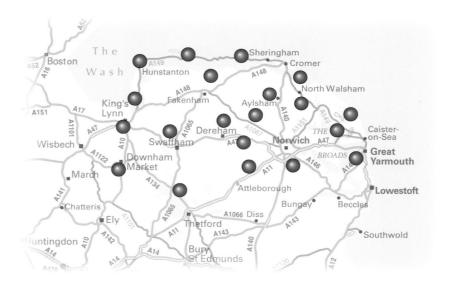

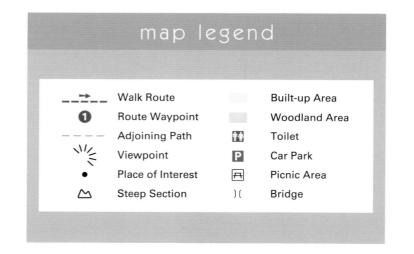

The Walks

The book includes a variety of walks, ranging from gentle ambles around nature reserves and other long distance trails. Some of the walks are exclusively on footpaths and include routes across farmland and meadows that can be gloriously muddy. Others are along surfaced country lanes that provide easy and level walking. Most walks will offer a combination.

Forays into Norfolk

There are four areas within Norfolk that are particularly worth a visit. First, no trip to the county would be complete without a foray into the Broads – one of England's best-known National Parks and a region of outstanding beauty. When walking around Horsey and Breydon, you will see picturesque lakes with windmills silhouetted on the horizon and boats dotted around the surface. Second, the sandy heaths and coniferous forests of Breckland add to Norfolk's special character, as you will see if you follow the route around Thetford and Downham Market. Third, few will deny that Norfolk's coast is a fabulous area to walk. There are miles of wide sandy beaches around Hunstanton, where the sea appears as a distant silver line on the horizon, and there are salty marshes that are full of reeds and grass that wave and hiss in the breeze at Brancaster and Burnham. And, finally, there is west Norfolk, where the Fens merge into marshland, a silent and lonely area where bird calls are the only sound.

These walks will allow you to sample the delights of all these fabulous areas, and hopefully encourage you to explore this wonderful county further.

using this book

Information Panels
An information panel for each walk shows its relative difficulty, the distance and total amount of ascent. An indication of the gradients you will encounter is shown by the rating ▲▲▲ (no steep slopes) to ▲▲▲ (several very steep slopes). The minimum time suggested for the walk is for reasonably fit walkers and doesn't allow for stops.

Suggested Maps
Each walk has a suggested Ordnance Survey Explorer map.

Start Points
The start of each walk is given as a six-figure grid reference prefixed by two letters indicating which 100-km square of the National Grid it refers to. You'll find more information on grid references on most Ordnance Survey maps.

Dogs
We have tried to give dog owners useful advice about the dog friendliness of each walk. Please respect other countryside users. Keep your dog under control, especially around livestock, and obey local bylaws and other dog-related notices.

Car Parking
Many of the car parks suggested are public, but occasionally you may find you have to park on the roadside or in a lay-by. Please be considerate when you leave your car, ensuring that access roads or gates are not blocked and that other vehicles can pass safely.

Maps
Each walk in this book is accompanied by a map based on Ordnance Survey information. The scale of these maps varies from walk to walk.

ABOVE: Sutton Mill, a windmill near the village of Stalham

ABOVE: The wide expanse of Holkham beach

*Visit a working mill and
a floodgate protecting
the Fens from tidal surges.*

Denver Sluice and the Fens

One of the Downham Market area's most famous sons was George William Manby, born at Denver Hall. In February 1807, Manby was in Great Yarmouth when HMS *Snipe* was wrecked on a nearby sand bar. All attempts to reach it failed and, despite heroic efforts by local people, all hands were drowned. This traumatic experience affected Manby deeply, and he decided to find a way to secure a stricken ship to the shore.

*ABOVE: The flood protection gates at the Denver Sluice
RIGHT: Denver Windmill, Downham Market*

The Innovative Mr Manby

Manby devised a manner in which a line could be connected to the shot fired from a mortar on shore to the ship. Then, to use that line to get stranded seamen ashore, he produced a small boat with a number of casks fixed as buoyancy chambers, developing the principle still used as a safety measure in small boats today. His apparatus was so successful that Parliament awarded him £2,000. Manby turned to a career as an inventor, including making harpoons and harpoon guns for the whaling industry.

Sluice Politics

Denver is famous for its sluices, as well as for Manby. The first sluice was built by Cornelius Vermuyden to limit the tidal flow up the Great Ouse. The Duke of Bedford, who funded the project, was delighted to see his lands become viable for farming, but not everyone shared his sentiments. The Fen Tigers were a group who did not want to see their way of life changed by drainage. They blew up the sluice to make their point.

Sailors and traders also resented the sluice, because it blocked the direct route to Cambridge and forced them to take their coal via Earith. It was destroyed again in 1713, this time by the sea, and was rebuilt several times before Sir John Rennie designed the one existing today. It was remodelled and new steel gates added in 1928, 1963 and 1983. The Denver Sluice (1959) stand on a newer waterway called the Relief Channel. The sluice are closed to prevent sea water rushing up the Great Ouse and opened to allow fresh water to drain the Fens. Without these gates and the pumping stations around the Fens the whole area would revert to marsh and flood plain.

Downham Market has a medieval church, indicating that it was here long before the Fens were drained. If you stand at the church you will see why: the settlement stands on a ridge above the surrounding marshes. Nevertheless, most of its important buildings date from much later.

walk directions

1 Leave the car park and turn right. When you reach Somerfield on your left, cut through its car park to a road running parallel to Paradise Road; turn right. The road winds downhill, passing the White Hart pub, to a level crossing and the station. Continue past Heygates flour mill on your left, and cross Hythe Bridge over the Great Ouse Relief Channel. On the far side of the bridge cross a stile on your right. Walk along a track to a junction of paths by the river bank.

2 Take the left-hand fork, and cross a second stile to reach the Fen Rivers Way along the east bank of the River Great Ouse. The banks have been raised to prevent flooding. After about 0.25 mile (400m) you reach a bridge.

3 Cross carefully over the busy A1122 and continue through a pair of gates to return to the river bank. The path then continues until you reach the lock at Salters Lode. Proceed until the Denver Sluice comes into sight.

4 After exploring the sluice, turn left along the lane and cross the bridge over the Relief Channel. Keep to the lane as it winds through farmland and across a level crossing. After passing a huge field on your right, look for the sails of Denver Windmill up ahead.

5 After visiting the mill, continue along the lane for 0.5 mile (800m), then turn left up Sandy Lane. The lane becomes a track, which you follow until it ends at the junction with the B1507.

6 Turn left and, after a few paces, you reach the A1122. Cross this road carefully to reach London Road, signposted to the town centre. Use the pavement on the left-hand side,

passing the police station on your right. Eventually you reach a mini-roundabout with a large Tesco supermarket on the left.

7 Keep straight ahead passing the town sign, then fork left past the war memorial and aim for the clock tower, walking along the High Street and through the market square to the Castle Hotel. Turn left at the hotel and walk down Paradise Road a few paces until you reach the car park.

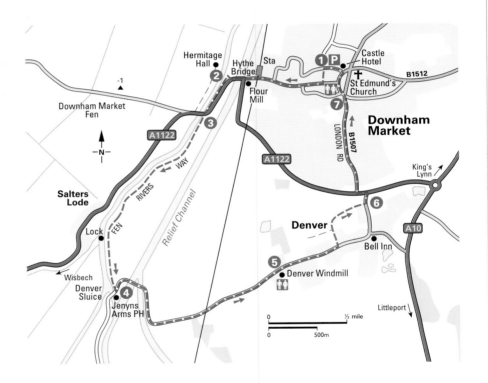

walk information

➤ **DISTANCE**	5.75 miles (9.2km)
➤ **MINIMUM TIME**	2hrs 30min
➤ **ASCENT/GRADIENT**	98ft (30m)
➤ **LEVEL OF DIFFICULTY**	
➤ **PATHS**	Riverside footpaths and country lanes, town streets, 2 stiles
➤ **LANDSCAPE**	Flat fenland, river and drainage channels, arable farmland
➤ **SUGGESTED MAPS**	OS Explorer 236 King's Lynn, Downham Market & Swaffham
➤ **START/FINISH**	Grid reference: TF 611033
➤ **DOG FRIENDLINESS**	Keep dogs under control along river bank (livestock)
➤ **PARKING**	Free Town Council car park in Paradise Road
➤ **PUBLIC TOILETS**	Beside Town Hall in Market Square

*Follow cobbled lanes to
King's Lynn's museums,
the river and a ferry ride.*

King's Lynn: A Port on a Silty River

King's Lynn was originally just called Lynn, and was an unassuming little place. But in the early Middle Ages, things began to take off. Lynn was strategically placed on one of the most important waterways in medieval England and soon a huge amount of trade was passing through. It exported corn from Lincolnshire, lead from Derbyshire, salt from Norfolk and Lincolnshire and, most importantly, wool from the East Midlands. It imported dried cod from Iceland and timber, pitch and resin from the Baltic, as well as Flemish and Italian cloths.

*ABOVE: The King's Lynn Guildhall was built in 1410
RIGHT: The Custom's House (centre-right) at Kings Lynn*

A Chequered History

With all these revenues, Lynn became a wealthy place, and Herbert de Losinga, the first Bishop of Norwich, decided he wanted it for himself. It became known as Bishop's Lynn, and so remained until the 1530s, when Henry VIII squashed its ecclesiastical association and named it King's Lynn, after himself. The change in name meant little to Lynn's merchants, who remained prosperous and continued to build their grand houses and churches, many of which can still be seen today.

King's Lynn is an architectural dream, with almost every period represented, ranging from St Nicholas's Chapel, built between 1145 and 1420, to picturesque Burkitt Court Almshouses, built in 1909 in memory of a Lynn corn merchant. One of the most visible landmarks is the Greyfriars Tower, which was part of a Franciscan Friary and was built in the 14th century. The beautifully proportioned Custom House is now a tourist information centre and was originally built in 1683 as a merchants' exchange.

St George's Guildhall is the largest surviving guildhall in England. It was built around 1410, and has been used as a warehouse, a store for guns during the Civil War and a court house. It is now the King's Lynn Arts and houses an art gallery, a theatre and a coffee shop.

Not all of Lynn's history has been a tale of success and prosperity. The town suffered during the Civil War, when Cromwell's Parliamentarians besieged the Royalist troops stationed here. In 1643 a cannon ball went through the west window of St Margaret's Church. The town also endured terrible floods, and the water levels are marked near the west door of St Margaret's. King's Lynn is a charming town for walks laden with history, exploring parks and gardens, and perusing the shops and finding a bite to eat.

walk directions

1 From the car park, head for King's Lynn Auction Rooms, pass the fitness centre and swimming pool and cross the road to the park. Take the path towards the chapel of St John the Evangelist.

2 Turn right by the pond. On a little knoll to your left is the red-brick Chapel of Our Lady of the Mount, built in 1485 for pilgrims travelling to Walsingham. When you reach the ruinous walls of the town's defences, continue on the path straight ahead with the football ground to your left.

3 Keep straight ahead into Guanock Terrace, passing The Beeches guest house and Lord Napier pub to the statue of Mayor Frederick Savage. Bear left at London Road to 15th-century South Gate, then cross the road to the Honest Lawyer guest house. Walk past South Gate and turn right at the roundabout. Cross a bridge over the River Nar and take the unmarked path to the right immediately after the bridge.

4 This is the final stretch of the Nar Valley Way, which follows the river to the Nar Outfall Sluice, where it meets the Great Ouse. Clamber up the bank and take the path to the left along the east river bank. After 0.75 mile (1.2km), turn right over the bridge.

5 Turn right on the far side of the bridge on to the Fen Rivers Way. Follow this path for just over a mile (1.6km), with views across the river to King's Lynn. Initially, the path is grassy, but then becomes a boardwalk leading to the ferry station.

6 Take the ferry (runs every 20 minutes from 7am to 6pm, not Sundays) back to King's Lynn. Walk up Ferry Lane as far as King Street. Turn left to see the Tuesday Market Place with its 750-seat Corn Exchange concert hall.

7 Retrace your steps past Ferry Lane and continue to Purfleet Quay, which houses the Custom House and a statue of explorer George Vancouver, Lynn's most famous son. At the end of the quay, cross

walk information

➤ **DISTANCE**	4 miles (6.4km)
➤ **MINIMUM TIME**	2hrs (allow longer for museums)
➤ **ASCENT/GRADIENT**	Negligible
➤ **LEVEL OF DIFFICULTY**	
➤ **PATHS**	Pavements, cobbled streets, grassy river path and steps to ferry (operates all year but not on Sundays)
➤ **LANDSCAPE**	Town buildings and open riverside
➤ **SUGGESTED MAPS**	OS Explorer 250 Norfolk Coast West Ashdown
➤ **START/FINISH**	Grid reference: TF 620199
➤ **DOG FRIENDLINESS**	Dogs can roam free, but watch for traffic in town
➤ **PARKING**	Blackfriar Street car park or St James multi-storey (pay-and-display)
➤ **PUBLIC TOILETS**	At car park and various locations in town

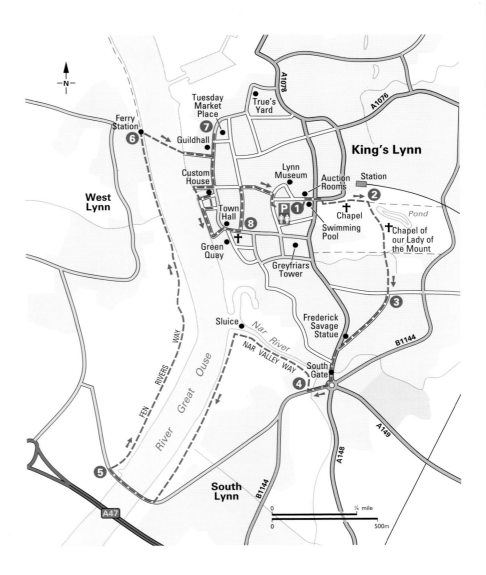

the bridge and take a narrow lane opposite to reach cobbled King's Staithe Lane. Turn right to return to the river bank, then head left to Thorseby College, built in 1500 for 13 chantry priests. Turn left to walk along College Lane to reach the Saturday Market Place, with the Town House Museum to your left. Bear right and then left, passing the attractive chequered Town Hall and Old Gaol House with St Margaret's Church dominating the square.

8 Turn left on to the pedestrian High Street for a flavour of the modern town. At the crossroads, turn right along New Conduit Street, then right again on Tower Street. Take the alley to the left opposite the Majestic Cinema to return to the car park.

PERSIMMON
SIRE ST·SIMON — FOALED 1893 — DAM PERDITA II
1895   1896   1897
THE COVENTRY STAKES   THE DERBY STAKES   THE ASCOT GOLD CVP
ASCOT   TIME 2MIN 42.SEC   THE ECLIPSE STAKES
THE RICHMOND STAKES   THE ST LEGER STAKES   TRAINED BY   R.MARSH
GOODWOOD   THE JOCKEY CLVB   STVD GROOM   E.WALKER
                                                RIDDEN BY   J.WATTS

*A stately home, country park,
historic railway station and
nature reserves on a forest stroll.*

Sandringham and Wolferton

*ABOVE: The garden at Sandringham,
leading towards the house
LEFT: A statue of Edward VII's Derby-winning
horse, Persimmon, at the Royal
Stud, Sandringham*

n 1862, revenues from the Duchy of Cornwall had raised such a large sum of money for its owner, the Prince of Wales – the future King Edward VII – that he was able to buy himself a fine house. He chose Sandringham, some 7,000 acres (2,835ha) of beautiful rolling countryside. The house, however, was not at all to his liking, so he set about rebuilding it in a style he felt reflected his status. The result was the rambling Jacobean-style palace in red brick and stone that you can visit today – providing that no member of the Royal Family wants to stay in it, of course.

Sandringham Country Park

Today it is the private property of the Queen, along with much of the surrounding countryside. In 1968, she expressed the wish that the general public should also enjoy the estate and some 600 acres (243ha) of woodland and open heath were set aside as the Sandringham Country Park. Access to the park is free (there is a charge to enter Sandringham Gardens) and visitors can enjoy the peaceful waymarked nature trails, as well as the observation hide to watch the wildlife around Jocelyn's Wood nature reserve. Visitors to the house and its gardens can also see some of the most spectacular parkland in the country, with an intriguing mixture of formal arrangements and ancient rambling woodland.

A Station Fit for Kings

When Sandringham was owned by the fun-loving Prince of Wales, the unassuming little railway station at nearby Wolferton saw some of the world's most powerful monarchs and statesmen pass through the station. Consequently, in 1898 the track from King's Lynn was upgraded and two staterooms added to the station, so that visiting dignitaries could arrive in style. When the railways came under the axe in the 1960s, Wolferton looked set to follow the fate of many other small stations, but one British Rail inspector was so impressed by what he saw that he decided to buy it.

Painstaking restoration slowly took place and the waiting rooms were converted into a museum, with exhibits about what it was like to travel in Victorian and Edwardian times. Unfortunately, the Sandringham estate refused permission for the museum to put up any advertising signs, so in 2001 the owner decided to sell it. Although since purchased as a private house, the fabric of the station is still the same and, at the moment, the pretty rust-red ironstone station, easily seen from the road, is close to how it might have looked in the 19th century. There are no tracks, and flowers enjoy the place where grunting, hissing steam engines would once have stood, but it is an atmospheric place and it is easy to imagine the bustle and commotion of its former life.

RIGHT: The Jacobean-style Sandringham House is set in 60 acres of gardens

ABOVE: A tunnel of lime trees at Sandringham

walk directions

1 Cross the road from the car park and bear right on the lane towards Wolferton. The walled gardens of the Old Rectory mark the end of the mixed woodland. Continue straight ahead at the junction, past St Peter's Church. The road bends to the right, passing the old railway gatehouse and cottages (1881) bearing the fleur-de-lis emblem. Stay on this road to make a complete circuit of the village, eventually arriving at Wolferton Station.

2 After the station, follow the road to the left and go up a hill until you reach the car park for the Dersingham nature reserve and a gate beyond it.

3 Go through the gate and take the track to your left, signed 'Wolferton Cliff and Woodland Walk'. The path climbs to a cliff top looking out over a forest, which 6,000 years ago was the seabed (now 1.5miles/2.4km distant). Follow the track until you see the 330yd (302m) circular boardwalk around the bog to go down some steps to your left. Walk down the steps to explore the bog walk. Emerging from the boardwalk, take the sandy track to your left, skirting the woods to return to Scissors Cross. Take the left fork out of the car park and walk along this road to the A149.

4 Cross the A149 and take the lane opposite, passing a house named The Folly. After a few paces you will see a lane to your left marked 'scenic drive'. Turn left to walk through the gates.

5 Walk along the drive or take the footpath on the right through Sandringham Country Park. When you see a processional avenue leading to Sandringham House on your right, leave the drive and look for a gap in the trees to your left. Follow the trail past a bench and down some steps, then stay on the yellow trail (waymarked in the opposite direction) as it winds through Jocelyn's Wood before returning to the main drive. Turn left and walk along the drive to the car park and visitor centre.

6 From the visitor centre, head for the lower car park and pick up the yellow trail again, which follows the main road, but is tucked away behind the trees of Scotch Belt. Cross a lane, then take the road ahead to your left for 200yds (183m) before picking up the path on your right as it passes through Brickkiln Covert.

7 At the crossroads, where the footpath comes to an end, turn right down a quiet lane with wide verges. You are still in woodland, although the trees here tend to be silver birch rather than the oaks and pines seen earlier. Cross the A149 to reach Scissors Cross.

walk information

➤ **DISTANCE**	6.5 miles (10.4km)
➤ **MINIMUM TIME**	3hrs
➤ **ASCENT/GRADIENT**	131ft (40m) ▲▲▲
➤ **LEVEL OF DIFFICULTY**	🚶🚶🚶
➤ **PATHS**	Marked forest trails and country lanes, some steps
➤ **LANDSCAPE**	Country park and woodland nature reserve
➤ **SUGGESTED MAPS**	OS Explorer 250 Norfolk Coast West
➤ **START/FINISH**	Grid reference: TF 668280
➤ **DOG FRIENDLINESS**	Dogs should be kept on lead in nature reserves
➤ **PARKING**	Scissors Cross car park on road to Wolferton
➤ **PUBLIC TOILETS**	At Sandringham visitor centre

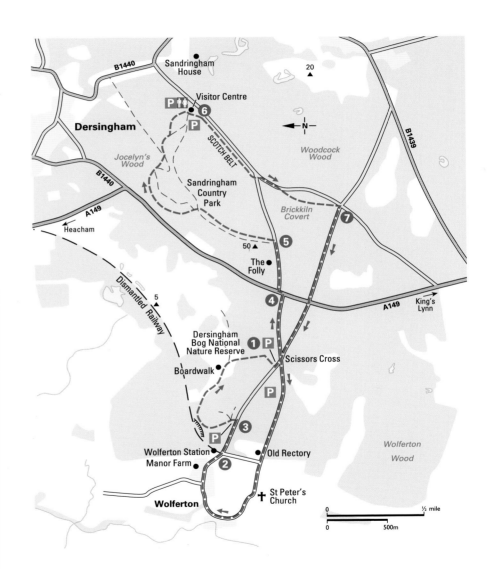

From the coast's wide-open magnificence to a peaceful nature reserve.

A Saint's Tale in Old Hunstanton

ABOVE: The present lighthouse on the cliffs at Hunstanton was built in 1844
LEFT: Sunset on Hunstanton beach

Old Hunstanton is steeped in history and legend. It is said that St Edmund was shipwrecked here in AD 855, and was so grateful for being spared a watery death in the Wash that he built a chapel as an act of thanksgiving. The 13th-century ruins still stand today, looking out across grey stormy seas from near the old lighthouse. Edmund left Hunstanton soon after and went on to become King of the East Angles. Between AD 869 and 870 Vikings invaded his kingdom and fought battles until he was captured.

The Miracle of St Edmund

Some years after refusing to renounce his faith and suffering a particularly unpleasant death, Edmund's grave was dug up and his body was found to be uncorrupted. It was declared a miracle and his remains were moved around the country for many years in an attempt to keep them safe from Vikings. They were eventually kept in Bury St Edmunds, although records are vague about what happened to them later. Some say they were taken to France, while others claim he was reinterred at Bury after the Reformation. Regardless of the fate of the relics, Hunstanton is still proud of its claim to a small piece of the saint's history.

Antics in the Wash

Edmund is not the only remarkable historical figure to be associated with the village. Members of the Le Strange family have been squires and landlords here for more than 800 years. They laid claim to the beach and, according to one charter, all that is in the sea for as far as a horseman can hurl a spear at low tide. The family still hold the title of Lord High Admiral of the Wash. There is a popular local story that tells of a famous German lady swimmer called Mercedes Gleitze performing the impressive feat of swimming the Wash from Lincolnshire to Norfolk in the 1930s and the admiral promptly stepping forward to claim her as his rightful property!

Listening Posts and Smugglers' Tales

The lighthouse that has become a symbol of this attractive town dates from 1830. When the First World War broke out in 1914, the light was extinguished and was never lit again. The lighthouse is now in private hands. Because of its strategic position on the coast, Hunstanton was the site of some very clandestine happenings in that war. Hippesley Hut, a bungalow, was used to house a secret listening post to monitor the activities of German Zeppelins and some of its secrets remain hidden even today.

Before you leave the village, spare a thought for poor William Green, a Light Dragoon officer, who was shot here in 1784 by smugglers while helping the King's customs men. The killers were never brought to justice, although the villagers, being such a small community, must have known their identities. The association of the village with contraband can be seen in the name Smugglers' Lane, along which you will walk.

walk directions

1 Walk towards the sea and turn left to head across the dunes. This is Norfolk at its best, with miles of sandy beaches and dunes, and the lighthouse at Old Hunstanton visible on a cliff. Keep close to the golf course and after about a mile (1.6km) you will arrive at a colourful row of beach huts.

2 When you see a gap in the fence to your left, take the path across the golf course and continue straight ahead into Smugglers' Lane. Emerging at a junction, take the lane opposite, past the post box to reach Caley Hall Hotel. Cross the A149 and aim for the road signed 'To St Mary's Church', where you can see the grave of William Green.

3 Turn right up Chapel Bank, through a tunnel of shade before reaching open farmland. After 700yds (640m), turn left on a grassy track, Lovers Lane, a permissive path. When you reach Lodge Farm, follow the track around farm buildings to a lane.

4 Turn left along the route marked Norfolk County Council Ringstead Rides. When you see the fairy-tale lodge of Hunstanton Park ahead, follow the lane round to the right along an avenue of mature trees. In the field to your right you will see the ruins of 13th-century St Andrew's Chapel.

5 Bear left at Downs Farm and head for the gate to enter Ringstead Downs Nature Reserve, one of just a few areas in Norfolk that is chalk rather than sand. It belongs to the Norfolk Wildlife Trust and the area

walk information

➤ **DISTANCE**	8 miles (12.9km)
➤ **MINIMUM TIME**	3hrs 30min
➤ **ASCENT/GRADIENT**	164ft (50m) ▲▲ ▲
➤ **LEVEL OF DIFFICULTY**	👤👤 👤👤
➤ **PATHS**	Country tracks, lanes, muddy paths and sand dunes, 1 stile
➤ **LANDSCAPE**	Sandy beaches, rolling chalk valleys and farmland
➤ **SUGGESTED MAPS**	OS Explorer 250 Norfolk Coast West
➤ **START/FINISH**	Grid reference: TF 697438
➤ **DOG FRIENDLINESS**	On lead in nature reserves and on farmland
➤ **PARKING**	Beach car park at Holme next the Sea (pay at kiosk)
➤ **PUBLIC TOILETS**	By beach car park

is grazed by traditional hill sheep. This is one of the most beautiful parts of the walk. Follow the path right through the reserve until you reach a lane.

6 Turn left into Ringstead, where the tower of St Peter's Church still stands. Stay on this road as it bends right and left through the village, passing The Gin Trap Inn. The road climbs gently out of the village, forking right then left along Peddars Way towards a sail-less windmill.

7 At the last house, look for the waymarked path to the left. This cuts across a field, then turns right into a lovely tunnel of hedges. Note the Norfolk Songline sculpture half-way along the path.

8 Cross the A149 and walk through Holme village, with its long green to reach the car park.

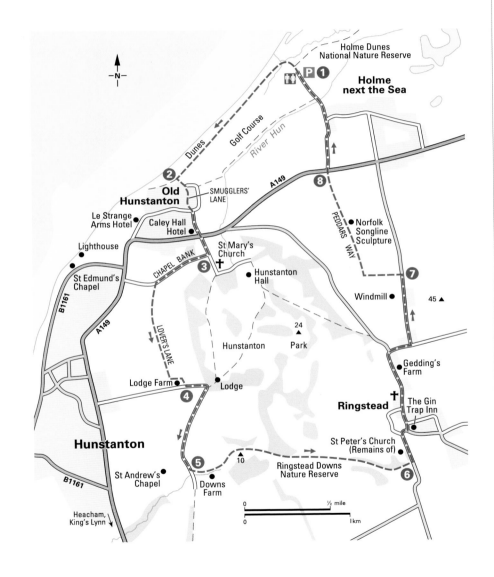

PAGE 30-31: The eroding cliffs at Hunstanton

A walk between Castle Acre and West Acre, once dominated by priories.

Priories and Castle Acre

Castle Acre Priory was the proud owner of the severed arm of St Philip, which generated a constant stream of generous pilgrims during medieval times. Folk came from near and far to pay homage to the relic, and to ask for boons and cures, and most left a gift of some kind behind. This made the priory wealthy, along with an Indulgence granted by Pope Boniface IX in 1401, which saw even more penitents arriving at its doors. But interest in relics and pilgrimages waned and, by 1533, the revenue from visitors to the priory was down to a mere ten shillings per year.

ABOVE: A village sign featuring Castle Acre Priory
RIGHT: A flock of sheep and their lambs rest near the ruins of the Priory

A Magnificent Priory

Revenues at the priory started to dwindle by the 1530s and when the last prior signed away his monastery to Henry VIII, it went mostly unnoticed. The site had a number of owners until it eventually came into the care of English Heritage.

During its heyday, Castle Acre Priory was one of the finest monasteries in East Anglia, and even today, when most of it comprises crumbling ruins and the foundations of walls in the grass, it is impressive. The site was enormous and was basically a self-contained village. It had bakeries and kitchens, pantries, butteries and wine cellars, and even its own brewery. Standing proudly amid all this was the priory church, and you can see how grand it must have been by looking at its magnificent west front today. Its dimensions are cathedral-like, with some of the most ornate carving anywhere in the county. There were also dormitories and refectories, and – something children seem to find fascinating – a long, multi-seated latrine over a small stream that provided some fairly respectable sanitary arrangements compared to those at the castle down the road.

Trouble at Acre

The castle at Acre came first, and there was a fort here long before the Normans built their sturdy motte, bailey and stone keep. The castle was built by William de Warenne, a baron who married one of William the Conqueror's daughters. He and Gundreda visited the great abbey at Cluny in Burgundy and, when they returned to England, they decided to found a Cluniac house at Lewes in Sussex. Castle Acre was founded as a daughter priory to Lewes, and was richly endowed.

Trouble soon erupted between the monks at Castle Acre and those at the Chapter General in Cluny. Cluny wanted power over its daughter, but the Norfolk clerics resisted. Things came to a head in 1283, when Prior William discovered that he had been replaced by Benedict of Cluny. William fortified Castle Acre Priory to keep the detested Benedict out. It's easy to imagine poor Benedict standing outside while you explore these remains.

1 From the green, walk along the lane past St James' Church until you reach the entrance to the priory. Turn right and then left, after a few paces, down the footpath signed 'Nar Valley Way'. Continue until you reach a pond.

2 At the pond, turn left and go through the kissing gate along the trail waymarked with a white disk. Walk through the meadow, with the River Nar to your left and enter a wood. Keep to this grassy track, continuing through the wood until you reach a gate. Cross the footbridge and keep straight ahead to another footbridge over the River Nar, with the old Mill House on your left. When you reach a lane with a ford on your right, go straight across to the path opposite and walk along a woodland track, looking for glimpses of West Acre priory ruins ahead.

3 Turn left by the circular waymarker sign and then follow the footpath for 0.25 mile (400m) until you reach a lane. Cross the lane and take the footpath opposite (not the bridleway on your left). Go up a hill, under power lines and past a wood. At the crest of the hill you reach a crossroads.

4 Turn left on to the bridleway and continue straight ahead at two crossroads. Look for deer and shy game birds, and note the prairie-style fields to the left and right.

5 Turn left at the third crossroads, on to an ancient drove road used in Roman times, passing Bartholomew's Hills Plantation on your right. Keep walking uphill along this sandy track until you see Castle Acre Priory and St James' Church through the trees ahead. As you descend, go under the power lines again, and meet a lane at the foot of the hill.

6 Go straight ahead on the lane, which is part of the Peddars Way. At the next junction go straight on again, down the lane marked

walk information

➤ **DISTANCE**	6.5 miles (10.4km)
➤ **MINIMUM TIME**	2hrs 45min
➤ **ASCENT/GRADIENT**	230ft (70m) ▲▲▲
➤ **LEVEL OF DIFFICULTY**	🚶🚶🚶
➤ **PATHS**	Footpaths, trackways and some tiny country lanes, can be very muddy, nettles, some steps
➤ **LANDSCAPE**	Wooded river valley, open fields
➤ **SUGGESTED MAPS**	OS Explorer 236 King's Lynn, Downham Market & Swaffham
➤ **START/FINISH**	Grid reference: TF 817151
➤ **DOG FRIENDLINESS**	Can run free but should be on lead on farmland
➤ **PARKING**	On road by village green, Castle Acre
➤ **PUBLIC TOILETS**	Priory Road, near entrance to Castle Acre Priory

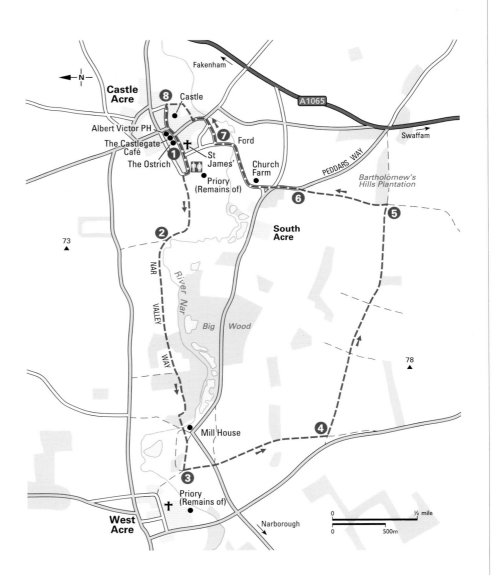

'Unsuitable for Motors'. Walk past Church Farm on your right to reach a pebble-bottomed river and a ford. Through the trees you will glimpse splendid views of the priory to your left. Cross the river and continue walking along this tiny lane until you see an acorn sign marking the route of Peddars Way.

7 Turn right along the Peddars Way and keep walking straight ahead until you see a sign for Blind Lane. Turn left at the junction, then right into Cuckstool Lane with the castle to your left. Follow the grassy path, which skirts around the castle bailey, climbing steeply to arrive at a lane.

8 Turn left and walk along the lane, past the old castle gate, to the village green.

*Walk along the pine-carpeted paths
of Thetford Forest, from a metal
stag to a mock-Jacobean hall.*

Lynford's Stag and Arboretum

*ABOVE: The ruins of Thetford Priory where
the Dukes of Norfolk were buried
in the Middle Ages
LEFT: An avenue of trees in Thetford Forest*

By 1916, with the First World War in full swing, the British government realised that it could no longer rely on timber imports to supplement Britain's own wood production and sustain industrial output. The huge demands placed on woodland resources by the onset of trench warfare and the spiralling need for colliery pit props brought the realisation that it would have to establish a group responsible for planting strategic timber reserves, as well as chopping them down again; the Forestry Commission was the solution.

Thetford Forest

The Forestry Commission was established immediately after the war in 1919. It began by buying up large tracts of land that were suitable for growing trees. One of the first areas it obtained was the sandy heathland around the ancient priory town of Thetford, because this was an ideal habitat for many species of fast-growing conifers.

By 1935, the new Thetford Forest had reached the boundaries on today's maps. It covers an area of approximately 50,000 acres (20,250ha), and is the largest lowland pine forest in the country. Originally, it was dominated by Scots pine, but this was changed to Corsican pine, which allows some 220,000 tons (224,000 tonnes) of timber to be cut every year. This is enough to build a 4ft (1.2m) high plank fence around the entire length of Britain's mainland coast. The amount taken is carefully controlled, so that the timber industry is sustainable – it never takes more than it plants.

Wildlife

The forest is more than just a giant timber-producing yard, however. It is home to numerous rare animals, birds and plants, including the native red squirrel, and people travel from miles around to enjoy the peace of the great forest trackways. Lucky visitors who walk quietly may spot one of the park's four species of resident deer: fallow, roe, red and muntjac. It is also home to a large number of bats, including the pipistrelle and the barbastelle, that feed on the many insects that inhabit the forest. Because the area is so important to bats, a bat hibernaculum has been built, to give them somewhere to spend the daylight hours.

Unusual Target

Lynford Stag is named for the life-sized metal deer that stands quietly and unobtrusively among the car parks and picnic benches. This was discovered by Forestry Commission workers when they were clearing the area for planting trees, and must have given them quite a surprise. It was made for Sir Richard Sutton, a keen hunter who owned nearby Lynford Hall. He used it for target practice and, if you approach it, you will see the scars of its previous existence.

Lynford Hall

Lynford Hall is a Grade II listed mock-Jacobean mansion standing amid imposing gardens overlooking a series of artificial lakes. The building began in 1857 on the site of an earlier hall dating to the 1720s. The estate was known for the splendid quality of its hunting, and birds and beasts continued to fall until 1924, when the hall was sold to the Forestry Commission. In the late 1940s, trainee foresters began to plant trees in its grounds. These now form the arboretum.

walk directions

1 Leave the car park by the metal stag and follow the blue marker posts into the trees. Jig slightly to the right and follow the markers heading north. The path then turns left. Take the next wide track to your right, next to a bench, leaving the blue trail to walk along the edge of the Christmas tree plantation. Eventually, you reach a paved road.

2 Cross the road and continue ahead on what was once part of the driveway leading to Lynford Hall. Pass a car park and a noticeboard with a map of forest trails. Continue ahead along a gravel path, picking up the next set of blue and green trails. The Church of Our Lady of Consolation is behind the trees to your right. It was designed by Pugin in the 1870s for the Catholic owner of the hall, but the next owner, a Protestant, planted trees to shield it from view. Shortly, reach a stone bridge.

3 Turn right and follow the gravel path along the shore of Lynford Lakes with views across the water to Lynford Hall. Turn left across a bridge to enter Lynford Arboretum and follow the path through the arboretum until you reach a road.

4 Turn left along the road, passing Lynford Hall Hotel on your left. After you have walked past the building, turn left through the main entrance gates of the hotel and walk up the drive.

5 When you see a sculpture of two bulls fighting, turn right on to a wide grassy sward called Sequoia Avenue. Walk almost to the end of it, then follow the blue markers to the left into the wood. After a few paces you come to the lake. The blue trail bears to the left at the end of the lake, but our walk continues straight ahead on the bridleway. The path jigs left, then right, but keep to the bridleway.

6 Cross a paved lane and continue straight on, towards the Christmas trees. Turn left at the end of the track, then almost immediately right, where you will pick up the blue trail markers again. Follow these until you reach the car park.

walk information

➤ DISTANCE	4.5 miles (7.2km)
➤ MINIMUM TIME	2hrs
➤ ASCENT/GRADIENT	66ft (20m)
➤ LEVEL OF DIFFICULTY	
➤ PATHS	Wide grassy trackways and small paths
➤ LANDSCAPE	Coniferous and mixed deciduous forest
➤ SUGGESTED MAPS	OS Explorer 229 Thetford Forest in The Brecks
➤ START/FINISH	Grid reference: TL 814917
➤ DOG FRIENDLINESS	On lead and keep away from children's play areas. No dogs (except guide dogs) in arboretum
➤ PARKING	Lynford Stag picnic site off A134
➤ PUBLIC TOILETS	Close to start

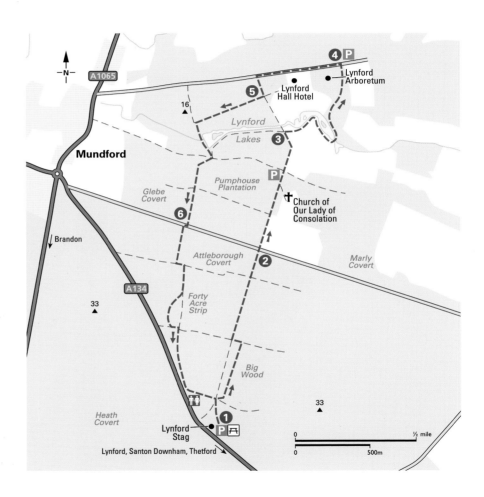

PAGE 40-41: Breckland Pine trees silhouetted against a dramatic orange sky at sunrise in Thetford

Tread in the footsteps of Nelson,

around the Burnham villages

and close to the marshes.

Burnham Thorpe's Hero

I n 1758 Edmund Nelson, rector of Burnham Thorpe, and his wife Catherine had the fifth of their 11 children and named him Horatio. The rectory where Horatio Nelson spent the first years of his life was demolished in 1802 and a new one built. However, when you visit Burnham Thorpe you will see a plaque set in a wall where the old rectory once stood.

ABOVE: The village sign for Burnham Market
LEFT: Boats at Burnham Overy Staithe

The Young Sailor

Nelson was just 12 when he entered the Royal Navy. He quickly gained experience, travelling as far afield as the Caribbean and the Arctic by the time he was 16. He went to India, but was sent home after contracting malaria. Throughout his travels he was plagued by seasickness, a fact in which many novice seamen find comfort. Nelson became a captain at the tender age of 20 and spent some years in the West Indies, where he enforced British law a little too vigorously for the Admiralty, who refused to give him another command until war broke out with France in 1792. During this frustrating time, Nelson lived in Burnham Thorpe with his wife Frances (Fanny). Once back in service he was sent to the Mediterranean, but was blinded in his right eye by splinters from a parapet struck by an enemy fire. Undaunted, he returned to duty the following day.

When he left the Mediterranean in 1797, Nelson's small fleet encountered a much larger French one. Due largely to his unusual tactics, the British inflicted an embarrassing defeat on the French, leading to a knighthood for Nelson. He lost his arm in the Canary Islands when trying to capture Spanish treasure and was wounded yet again in the Battle of the Nile – from which he emerged victorious. He was then nursed by Emma, Lady Hamilton, who later become his lover. Elevation to the peerage as Baron Nelson of the Nile followed.

His brazen affair with Lady Hamilton (who became pregnant with their daughter Horatia) led to an estrangement from his wife, and lack of money forced him to apply for active service again. His fleet engaged a hostile force near Copenhagen, where he refused to obey the order of a senior officer to disengage. The battle was won, along with further honours. Four years later, in 1805, he was fatally wounded at the battle of Trafalgar.

Although Nelson was buried in St Paul's Cathedral, there are plenty of reminders of him in the Burnhams. There is a bust of him above his father's tomb in 13th-century All Saints' Church, along with flags from his battles. Also on display in the church are the flags and ensigns from the Second World War battleship HMS *Nelson*. The Lord Nelson pub at Burnham Thorpe has a collection of memorabilia.

walk directions

1 From the centre of Burnham Overy Town and the broken Brothercross where villagers once traded their wares, follow Mill Road north as it bends round to the right. As the road bends again (this time to the left) turn right onto a track. Follow this track and its circular markers with yellow arrows until you reach a dirt lane. Cross the lane and head diagonally in a straight line across the field through gaps in hedges until you reach a waymarker at a field edge. Here, turn right and keep to left of the hedge until you get to a gap at the entrance to the field (marked as a footpath).

2 Turn right down the lane towards Burnham Thorpe. Large fields stretch away on either side until you reach the crossroads.

3 With Leath House to your right, continue past the houses into a shady lane, with orchards to the left and right, shielded from the bitter sea winds by hedges. Keep to the left at the first junction as you arrive into Burnham Thorpe, and take the road towards The Creakes at the second junction.

4 Here you'll find the best views of the valley of the River Burn. The road loops round to the right – go right at the T-junction and follow the sign to Nelson's birthplace, marked by a plaque on the wall. This was given to the village by one of his officers.

5 From here, take the footpath opposite the parsonage to follow the river for a while, then rejoin the lane towards Burnham Thorpe.

6 On reaching Burnham Thorpe, turn right on Garners Row. At the end of the street, go left to the Nelson sign, then right on to Lowes Lane to the lane that leads to All Saints' Church. The rood in the chancel arch is made up of timbers from Nelson's flagship at Trafalgar, HMS Victory.

PAGE 44-45: A sunset at Burnham Overy Staithe
LEFT: All Saints' Church at Burnham Thorpe

7 Where the lane bends left around the church, go through a kissing gate on to a footpath, across a meadow, with the river to your left. The path goes through another kissing gate, then crosses an old railway embankment, jinking left before heading north along a field-edge. Eventually, the path reaches a lane. Turn left and walk into Burnham Overy Town, towards the broken Brothercross.

walk information

➤ DISTANCE	3.5 miles (5.6km)
➤ MINIMUM TIME	2hrs
➤ ASCENT/GRADIENT	85ft (25m)
➤ LEVEL OF DIFFICULTY	
➤ PATHS	Waymarked paths
➤ LANDSCAPE	Wild salt marshes and mudflats, fields and meadows
➤ SUGGESTED MAPS	OS Explorer 251 Norfolk Coast Central
➤ START/FINISH	Grid reference: TF 843428
➤ DOG FRIENDLINESS	On lead in nature reserves and under control on farmland
➤ PARKING	On-street parking on main road in Burnham Overy Staithe, or off-road at the harbour
➤ PUBLIC TOILETS	None on route

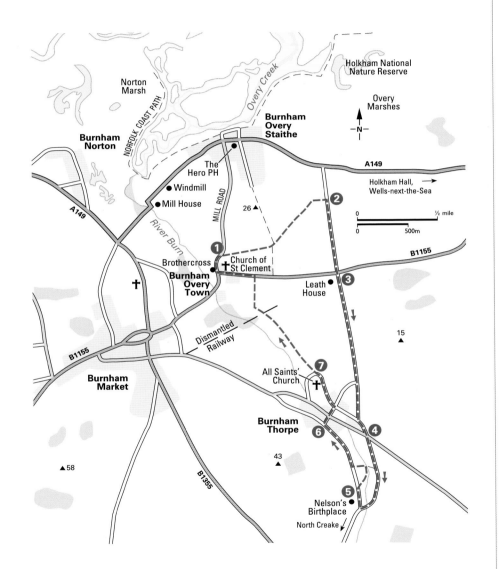

6/8/2010

Tread in the footsteps of pilgrims to one of the most important medieval shrines in England.

Barefoot to Walsingham

In the 11th century, Richeldis de Faverches was lady of the manor in Walsingham. One night, the Virgin Mary appeared in a dream telling her to build a copy of the Sancta Casa, the 'Holy House' in Nazareth where Mary had been visited by the Angel Gabriel. Richeldis was torn between two sites for the building, but work began immediately on one site and Ithough the men worked all day, little progress was made. However, it is said that the following morning, the house on the second site had been miraculously completed. This and other occurences contributed to Walsingham becoming one of the most important pilgrimage sites in the medieval world.

ABOVE: The church of St Mary in the village of Great Snoring dates from the 13th century
RIGHT: Timber-framed buildings front the road in Little Walsingham

A Thriving Site of Pilgrimage

The shrine at Walsingham did not remain a small house with two wells for long. As pilgrims flocked here, so did those in the service industry, and soon inns and guest houses for travellers were built. The Church arrived too and Franciscan friars and Augustinian canons built themselves priories. These were simple at first, but as more and more pilgrims arrived and left behind their pennies and their gifts, the priories became larger and more sumptuous. There was a handsome church for pilgrims to pray in and a special chapel for a statue of the Virgin, richly bedecked in jewels and fine cloth.

When the Holy Land was retaken by the Infidels after the crusades, it was rumoured that the Virgin Mary had abandoned her original shrine and had come to live in Norfolk instead. One tale even had it that the original Sancta Casa had magically uprooted itself from Nazareth and landed at Walsingham. The shrine was visited by paupers and kings alike, and many monarchs from Richard I to Henry VIII came to pay homage and to ask for favours. Walsingham's future seemed glitteringly assured.

The success of the village lasted for 500 years, until the Reformation. Henry VIII's dramatic reshuffling of the Church in England involved the destruction of many abbeys, priories and shrines, and Walsingham was among them. The two priories were torn down in the 1530s, so that only fragments remain, and papist practices such as worshipping statues of Mary were forbidden. Walsingham became just like any other village in Tudor England, and so it remained, almost forgotten by the outside world, until the 1930s, when Father Hope Patten revived the shrine.

Walsingham has come full circle, and is once again a thriving pilgrimage site. Visitors pour in by the thousand, to visit shrines considered holy by Anglicans and Catholics alike.

walk directions

1 Return to the main exit of the car park and turn left, soon to go down Coker's Hill. Go straight across at the junction along Back Lane. The remains of the Franciscan friary are to your left and have been incorporated into a private house. At a T-junction, turn right uphill, then where the lane curves right, go left along the Pilgrims' Way, the route of a dismantled railway.

2 Follow the level gravel path through open country with good views for 1 mile (1.6km). When it ends, turn left into Houghton St Giles and turn right to pass the Slipper Chapel on your left (built in the 1300s and partly destroyed during the Reformation), then past the former railway until you enter North Barsham.

3 At the junction, keep left, and take the lane signposted towards West Barsham, to reach a junction in a shady copse. Take the lane to the left, up the hill with a fir plantation on your right. Go down a hill, past more of the dismantled railway and eventually reaching the village of East Barsham.

4 Turn left at the T-junction and walk past the White Horse Inn. Just after passing a red-brick manor house, turn right into Water Lane, signed to Great Snoring. Look for partridges, yellowhammers and finches in the hedgerows.

5 At the junction, take the right-hand turn towards Thursford. (It is possible to take The Greenway to Walsingham shortly after this point, but be warned that it can be extremely boggy.) Continue ahead into Great Snoring, and turn left by the large red-brick house, then quickly reach open fields again. After a mile (1.6 km), look out for an arrowed path on the left and cross a stile into a field. Follow the worn path ahead, which soon curves left to a gate. Continue across pasture to a further stile and turn right along a drive, with the abbey ruins visible ahead. At the road, follow the path left along the back and into St Mary's churchyard.

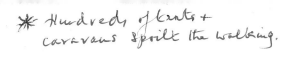
✳ Hundreds of tents + caravans spoilt the walking.

6 Exit St Mary's churchyard via the main gate and then continue walking along the road, turning right at the junction into Little Walsingham. To visit the Anglican shrine, turn right at the pumphouse, topped with a brazier that is lit on state occasions, otherwise keep ahead and then turn immediately left to reach the car park.

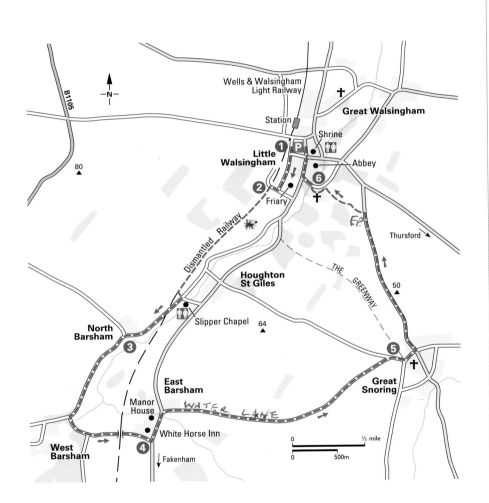

walk information

➤ **DISTANCE**	7.25 miles (11.7km)
➤ **MINIMUM TIME**	3hrs 45min
➤ **ASCENT/GRADIENT**	164ft (50m) ▲▲▲
➤ **LEVEL OF DIFFICULTY**	🚶🚶🚶
➤ **PATHS**	Mostly country lanes
➤ **LANDSCAPE**	Rolling agricultural scenery with meadows and woodland
➤ **SUGGESTED MAPS**	OS Explorer 251 Norfolk Coast Central
➤ **START/FINISH**	Grid reference: TF 933368
➤ **DOG FRIENDLINESS**	Dogs can run free along the former railway track
➤ **PARKING**	Pay-and-display car park in Little Walsingham
➤ **PUBLIC TOILETS**	At shrine and Slipper Chapel

Walk where Saxons prayed and Victorians built their railways.

North Elmham and the Saxon Cathedral

In the period often known as the Dark Ages, when Christianity was fighting to establish itself in England, the Saxons founded a cathedral at the small village of Elmham in Norfolk. This quickly became the most important religious centre in East Anglia and was the seat of bishops. It is even possible that Edmund, the King and martyr who was murdered by Viking raiders, was crowned here. So, from the year AD 800, or possibly slightly earlier, the bishops of East Anglia resided in North Elmham, running sees and managing their religious and secular affairs.

ABOVE: The ruins at North Elmham incorporate elements of a manor home built here in the 14th century
RIGHT: The outline of the ruined walls suggests evidence of a western tower

The Moving See

Around AD 866 the Danes arrived, and were said to have laid the place to waste, destroying not only the cathedral, but the settlement too, forcing the bishops to abandon Elmham for a safer place. The see was re-established in AD 955, and a new cathedral raised, possibly on the site of the old one, and these are the foundations that have been excavated and that can be seen today. Four years after the Norman Conquest, the see was moved again, this time to Thetford, where it remained until 1094. It was then decided Norwich was a far more prestigious place and the see was moved once more. This move, however, was permanent and the bishop still has his cathedra (or seat) in Norwich Cathedral today.

Norman Earthworks

The Saxon cathedral was probably a timber building – there are two separate accounts from the 13th century and both claim it was built of wood. Certainly archaeologists have discovered post holes, indicating a fairly basic structure. Unfortunately, one Bishop Despenser raised himself a fortified manor house here in the 14th century and the foundations of the Saxon cathedral are all mixed up with those of his house. There is a huge earthwork to the north-west of the site, but this is more likely to be a Norman motte (or castle mound) than a Saxon fortification. Because the remains are confusing, historians argue about what is what, with some claiming that the foundations we see today do not belong to the cathedral at all, but are part of a private chapel erected by Bishop Herbert de Losinga between 1091 and 1119.

We may never know what the Saxon cathedral looked like, but the Norman chapel is easier to make out. The transepts were similar to those at Norwich Cathedral and the abbey at Bury St Edmund, so they must date from after the Conquest. The north doorway is also Norman. The twin towers (often referred to prosaically as 'armpit towers') are an unusual feature to be found in England, although they appear in Germany in the first half of the 12th century. Wander around the ruins and decide for yourself what they once were.

1 Look around the site of the Saxon cathedral, then leave the way you entered. Turn left along a gravel track with North Elmham's parish church of St Mary's to your right. The path winds downhill with hedges on either side until you reach an old bridge with a disused railway running underneath it. Cross the bridge and look for the stile immediately to your left.

2 Walk through the gap beside the stile and descend the steps to reach the disused railway line. Turn right, and continue along the path until functional railway tracks appear. At this point the path moves away to the right, safely tucked to one side. After about 0.75 mile (1.2km) you reach County School Station. Cross the road and keep straight ahead, following blue arrows marking the Wensum Valley Walks and keeping the railway tracks to your left. Continue for another 0.75 mile (1.2km), past Blackhall Farm, until the footpath leaves the railway track and descends steps to the B1110.

3 Turn right and, when you reach the remains of a Victorian railway bridge, keep left, following the blue cycleway signs directing riders to King's Lynn and Fakenham. Walk on this quiet lane until you reach a T-junction. Turn left and continue to reach the next junction.

4 Turn right along a shady lane, passing pretty Ling Plantation on your left. Turn sharp left along Greatheath Road signposted to North Elmham, to reach the other edge of Ling Plantation. Walk along this lovely lane for a little more than 0.75 mile (1.2km), until you reach some scattered houses. Look for the footpath off to your right, opposite the track leading to Dale Farm on your left.

5 Take the footpath to the right, mostly a wide gravel track. Follow it around to the left behind some houses and then right, towards another small plantation. Head left into the woods, following the blue arrows. The path emerges on to the driveway to Elmham House and comes out on the B1110 by an old red telephone box and posting box. This is North Elmham's High Street. Opposite you will see Millers Old Cottage.

6 Turn right along the High Street and walk until you see signs for the Saxon cathedral off to your left. Follow them back to the car park.

walk information

➤ **DISTANCE**	5.5 miles (8.8km)
➤ **MINIMUM TIME**	2hrs
➤ **ASCENT/GRADIENT**	115ft (35m)
➤ **LEVEL OF DIFFICULTY**	
➤ **PATHS**	Disused railway line and paved roads, some steps, one stile
➤ **LANDSCAPE**	Railway track and open woodland and farmland
➤ **SUGGESTED MAPS**	OS Explorer 238 Dereham & Aylsham
➤ **START/FINISH**	Grid reference: TF 988216
➤ **DOG FRIENDLINESS**	Dogs must be kept on lead on bridleways
➤ **PARKING**	Car park near Saxon cathedral in North Elmham village
➤ **PUBLIC TOILETS**	None on route

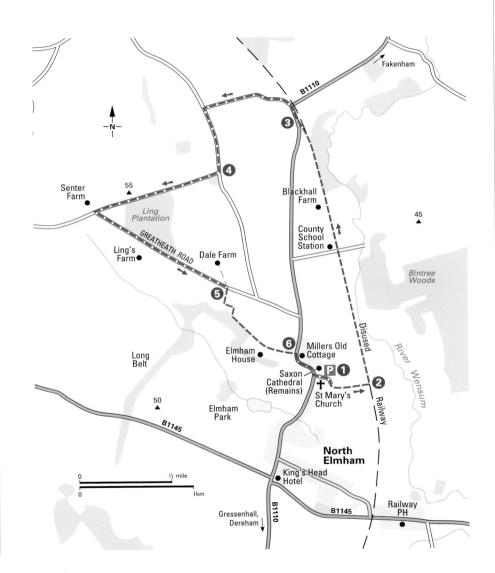

*Walk along the sea defences
to some of the finest bird
reserves in the country.*

Blakeney Eye's Magical Marshes

ABOVE: *A windmill stands on the riverbank
at Cley-next-the-Sea*
LEFT: *Fishing boats moored in
Blakeney harbour*

Blakeney was a prosperous port in medieval times, but went into decline when its sea channels began to silt up. However, although the merchants decried the slow accumulation of salt marsh and sand bars, birds began to flock here in their thousands. By Victorian times it had become a favoured spot shooting. Some sportsmen just wanted to kill the many waterfowl, while others were more interested in trophy collecting — looking for species that were rare or little-known. Many of these hapless birds ended up stuffed in museums or private collections.

Nature Reserve

After many years of bird shooting by visiting sportsmen, the National Trust arrived in 1912 and purchased the area from Cley Beach to the tip of the sand and shingle peninsula of Blakeney Point. It became one of the first nature reserves to be safeguarded in Britain. Today it is a fabulous place for a walk, regardless of whether you are interested in ornithology. A bright summer day will show you glittering streams, salt-scented grasses waving gently in the breeze and pretty-sailed yachts bobbing in the distance. By contrast, a wet and windy day in winter will reveal the stark beauty of this place, with the distant roar of white-capped waves pounding the beach, rain-drenched vegetation and a menacing low-hung sky filled with scudding clouds. Whatever the weather, a walk at Blakeney is always invigorating.

Although these days we regard the Victorians' wholesale slaughter of wildlife with distaste, they did leave a legacy of valuable information. It was 19th-century trophy hunters who saw the Pallas' warbler and the yellow-breasted bunting in Britain for the first time – and they were seen at Blakeney. A little later, when the Cley Bird Observatory operated here between 1949 and 1963, the first subalpine warbler in Norfolk was captured and ringed. .

The Victorians' records tell us that a good many red-spotted bluethroats appeared in September and October, and any collector who happened to visit then was almost certain to bag one. In the 1950s the observatory discovered that these were becoming rare at this time of year. Today, bluethroats are regular spring visitors but are seldom seen in the autumn. It is thought that this change over time is related to different weather patterns and indicates how climate change, even on this small scale, can dramatically effect the behaviour of birds.

RIGHT: The harbour and the surrounding marshes at Blakeney are owned by the National Trust

ABOVE: The village sign at Blakeney displays a seafaring history as well as the wildlife of the local area

1 From the car park head for the wildfowl conservation project, a fenced-off area teeming with ducks, geese and widgeon. A species list has been mounted on one side, so you can see how many you can spot. Take the path marked Norfolk Coast Path out towards the marshes. This raised bank is part of the sea defences, and is managed by the Environment Agency. Eventually, you have salt marshes on both sides.

2 At the turning, head east. Carmelite friars once lived around here, although there is little to see of their chapel, the remains of which are located just after you turn by the wooden staithe (landing stage) to head south again. This part of the walk is excellent for spotting kittiwakes and terns in late summer. Also, look for Sabine's gull, manx and sooty shearwaters, godwits, turnstones and curlews. The path leads you past Cley Windmill, built in 1810 and which last operated in 1919. It is open to visitors and you can climb to the top to enjoy the view across the marshes. Follow signs for the Norfolk Coast Path until you reach the A149.

3 Cross the A149 to the pavement opposite, then turn right. Take the first left after crossing the little creek. Eventually you reach the cobblestone houses of Wiveton and a crossroads; go straight ahead.

4 Take the grassy track opposite Primrose Farm, to a T-junction. This is Blakeney Road; turn right along it. However, if you want refreshments before the homeward stretch, turn left and walk a short way to the Wiveton Bell. The lane is wide and ahead you will see St Nicholas' Church nestling among trees. This dates from the 13th

century, but was extended in the 14th. Its two towers served as navigation beacons for sailors, and the east, narrower one is floodlit at night.

5 At the A149 there are two lanes opposite you. Take the High Street fork on the left to walk through the centre of Blakeney village. Many cottages are owned by the Blakeney Neighbourhood Housing Society, which rents homes to those locals unable to buy their own. Don't miss the 14th-century Guildhall undercroft at the bottom of Mariner's Hill. After you have explored the area, continue to the car park.

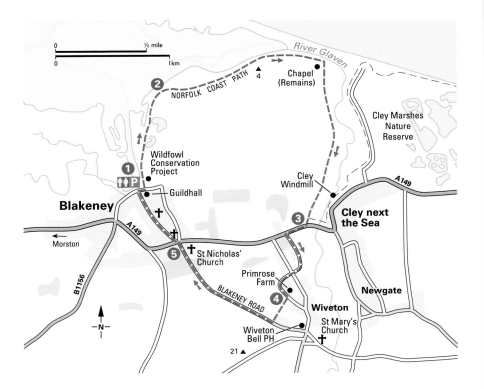

walk information

➤ **DISTANCE**	4.5 miles (7.2km)
➤ **MINIMUM TIME**	2hrs
➤ **ASCENT/GRADIENT**	98ft (30m)
➤ **LEVEL OF DIFFICULTY**	
➤ **PATHS**	Footpaths with some paved lanes, can flood in winter
➤ **LANDSCAPE**	Salt marshes, scrubby meadows and farmland
➤ **SUGGESTED MAPS**	OS Explorer 251 Norfolk Coast Central
➤ **START/FINISH**	Grid reference: TG 028442
➤ **DOG FRIENDLINESS**	Under control as these are important refuges for birds
➤ **PARKING**	Carnser (pay) car park, on seafront opposite Blakeney Guildhall and Manor Hotel
➤ **PUBLIC TOILETS**	Across road from Carnser car park

Wander in the steps of the diarist to five churches he knew and loved.

Mattishall and Parson Woodforde

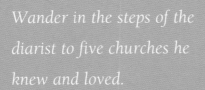

ABOVE: The Reverend James Woodforde (1740–1803)
LEFT: Detail from a stained glass window, All Saints Church, Mattishall (Artist: Ken Murrell)

In 1776, a 36-year-old parson arrived at the village of Weston Longville, north-east of Mattishall, and began to keep a diary. His name was James Woodforde and he continued to write his account of life in his parish, and other parishes to which he had occasion to visit, until his death in 1803. These were turbulent times: the colonists were rebelling in North America, King George III suffered bouts of insanity, the French Revolution was in full swing, Napoleon Bonaparte was moving across Europe and there were rebellions in Ireland. Yet none of these events worry the country parson. Woodforde was more interested in the activities of his parishioners than in world affairs.

Inebriated Pigs

In 1778 France joined the colonies against the British and the philosopher Voltaire died, but Woodforde wrote about how his two pigs got into a beer barrel and became intoxicated to the point where they were unable to stand. The poor beasts apparently remained inebriated the whole night, not even flinching when Woodforde 'slit their ears' to assess whether they could feel anything.

A Veritable Feast

In 1780, the year that the American Revolution saw the British fighting in Charleston and that anti-Catholic riots took place in London, Woodforde's diary for 28 January reads: 'We had for dinner a calf's head, boiled fowl and tongue, a saddle of mutton roasted on the side table, and a fine swan roasted with currant jelly sauce for the first course. The second course a couple of wild fowl called dun fowls, larks, blancmange, tarts etc, etc and a good dessert of fruit after amongst which was a damson cheese.'

He went on to comment that this was his first taste of swan, but that he did not consider it spoiled by the fact that it had been killed some three weeks previously. Perhaps this was due to the 'sweet sauce' that went with it. His diaries recount the daily happenings in the life of a comfortable 18th-century country parson who boasted a great many friends and a taste for good food. From Weston Longville, he visited all his neighbours in the parishes round about – Mattishall, North Tuddenham, East Tuddenham, Hockering, Honingham, Lyng and Elsing – and attended services in the churches you will see on this walk.

Woodforde's accounts went undiscovered until 1924, when they were published. The parishes that he knew have joined together to design the Eight Parishes Circular Walk, moving in the footsteps of the jolly parson as he ate and drank his way around the region. You will walk along part of the route on this delightful stroll as you visit this unspoiled part of Norfolk.

walk directions

1 Leave the car park and walk around the charming 14th-century All Saints' Church. Cross Dereham Road and head for Burgh Lane opposite. Walk up this, past the cemetery and through a residential area until you see Church Lane on your right. Walk down the lane to reach Mattishall Burgh's St Peter's Church (originally Norman, with later additions).

2 Leave the church and retrace your steps to Burgh Lane. Turn right and continue walking until you reach a T-junction. Turn left, following the signs to North Tuddenham. The lane narrows, and winds down a hill and up the other side. Keep going straight ahead until you reach an unpaved lane on your right after about 0.75 mile (1.2km).

3 Turn right and follow the track to charming 14th-century St Mary's Church, North Tuddenham. Retrace your steps to the paved lane, turn right and continue to another T-junction. Go right, along the lane signed to Hockering and Honingham. Stay on this lane past High Grove Farm and Two Acre Kennels, until you reach a crossroads.

4 Keep straight ahead as the lane narrows, aiming for the battlemented tower of Hockering's St Michael's Church (early 1300s). Cross the A47 carefully, and aim for the lane opposite. There is a notice board outside the church giving details of the Eight Parishes Project and Parson Woodforde.

5 Walk through the churchyard and look for two brick buttresses. Opposite these is a gate. Go through this, and the field ahead to reach the lane. Turn left, then right and recross the A47, aiming for the lane opposite and to your right, called Mattishall Lane. Turn left at the first junction.

6 Cross over a bridge, and keep left at the following junction called Blind Lane (not signed). Walk for about a mile (1.6km) until you reach a crossroads.

7 Go straight through the crossroads, walking down Church Lane until you reach Welborne. When you reach the junction, continue a few paces past the village hall to see All Saints' Church, which has a 12th-century round tower. Retrace your steps and turn left along Church Road, and then bear right at the next junction back towards Mattishall.

8 Turn right towards Mattishall at the end of Welborne Road, and keep walking until you reach Church Plain again.

walk information

➤ **DISTANCE**	7 miles (11.3km)
➤ **MINIMUM TIME**	2hrs 30min
➤ **ASCENT/GRADIENT**	131ft (40m) ▲▲▲
➤ **LEVEL OF DIFFICULTY**	🚶🚶🚶
➤ **PATHS**	Mostly paved country lanes
➤ **LANDSCAPE**	Gently rolling farmland
➤ **SUGGESTED MAPS**	OS Explorer 238 Dereham & Aylsham
➤ **START/FINISH**	Grid reference: TG 053110
➤ **DOG FRIENDLINESS**	Dogs can run free
➤ **PARKING**	At village square behind Mattishall church on Church Plain
➤ **PUBLIC TOILETS**	None on route

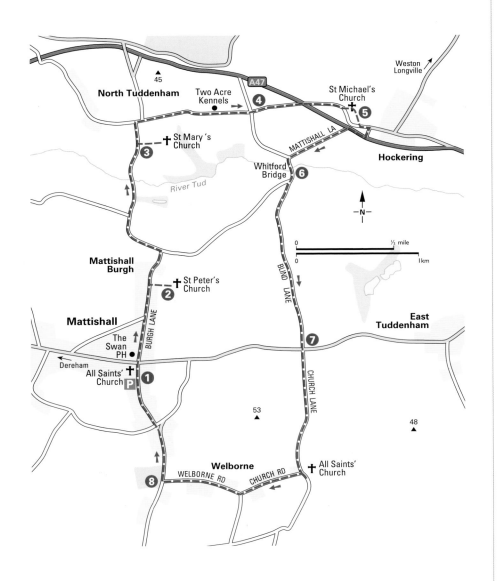

*Discover an abbey with
a long history in this
lovely market town*

Wymondham Figure of Eight

*ABOVE: The town sign of Wymondham
LEFT: Wymondham's Market Cross building
is used as a tourist information centre*

It is difficult to believe that peaceful Wymondham was once the site of a bitter dispute between its parishioners and the abbey's Benedictine monks. The two parties could not agree. They did not like the times when each other rang their bells and they did not like sharing the church. Matters came to a head in the 14th century, when the monks began to build a church tower, making it clear that this was going to be for their use only. In retaliation, in 1447, the townsfolk began to build their own tower – and then installed a peal of bells. The result is a church with two towers.

A Brief History of the Abbey

The dispute between the monks and the townsfolk dragged on for many years and was only laid to rest during the Dissolution, when the abbey buildings were destroyed and the monks expelled by Henry VIII. The people of Wymondham were allowed to keep the nave of the church, although they had to pay handsomely for it. The chancel, where the monks prayed, was demolished.

Today, the abbey church of St Mary and St Thomas of Canterbury is well worth a visit. The first thing you notice is that the grand central tower is nothing more than a shell, with the great arch that once led to the abbey buildings open to the elements. This was the monks' tower, completed in 1409. It effectively divided the church in half, and left the parishioners staring at a blank wall, while the monks enjoyed the chancel. The east wall remained blank until the screen was erected in the early 20th century.

Inside, the church is a delight. There are Norman arches in the nave and an angel roof, all drawing the eye forward to the gold extravaganza of the altar screen on the east wall. This was designed by Sir Ninian Comper and was begun in 1919. Plans had been mooted as early as 1911, but fundraising was suspended because of the First World War.

The monastery was originally founded in 1107 by William d'Albini, who also built the castle at New Buckenham and was Henry I's chief butler. The monastery was put under the stewardship of the great Benedictine abbey at St Albans. However, when the charters were drawn up, there was a certain amount of ambiguity about who had various rights, which led to the disputes of the 14th century. It became an abbey in 1448, the year after the parishioners started building their west tower.

RIGHT: The ruined Priory arch at Wymondham Abbey next to the Monks Tower (right)

walk directions

1 Exit car park on Market Street and turn left. To your right is the Market Cross (built in 1616) and now a Tourist Information Centre. At the bottom of the road is Church Street, leading past the chapel of Thomas Becket, founded in 1174. It is now a public library. Go past the 14th-century Green Dragon pub and the Hill House Hotel until you reach the abbey churchyard.

2 Exit the abbey churchyard through the gate by the north porch and turn right on to Becketswell Road, which becomes Vicar Street. Turn left at the war memorial, pass The Feathers pub and continue along Cock Street, then straight across the roundabout and up Chapel Lane. A few paces will bring you to an unmarked track on the left called Frogshall Lane. This gravel track leads past the backs of gardens, then narrows to a path, eventually reaching a kissing gate.

3 Pass through the gate. You are now entering the Tiffey Valley Project, where grazing pastures have been restored and managed using traditional methods. Cross the meadow to a kissing gate and a wooden footbridge across the river, then turn left and walk along the stream bank with views of the abbey across the meadows. Pass Wymondham Abbey station (Mid-Norfolk Railway) and cross the road to Becketswell Nature Reserve. Walk through the reserve and continue alongside the river to arrive at a bridge.

4 Turn right along White Horse Street, then cross the B1172 and head for Cemetery Lane. Walk along the lane, passing the cemetery and prize-winning Wymondham railway station, to arrive at an industrial estate.

5 Cross the main road and head left of the Railway pub to pass under a railway bridge.

LEFT: The Market Cross in Wymondham was built in 1616

6 After passing a row of houses, look for a path on the left leading to the Lizard, a conservation area that derives its name from an old English word for open fields.
A boardwalk takes you across the meadow to where steps lead up to a disused railway embankment. Turn right, walk along the embankment and descend more steps, and walk towards a gate.

7 Go through the gate and cross a meadow, turning right when you pass a second gate. The path leads along the hedge, then crosses the meadows and exits the nature reserve by a gate. Walk along the road to return to the railway bridge. When you reach the main road, turn right up Station Road to the traffic lights, then cross and walk along Fairland Street, back to Market Street and the car park.

walk information

➤ **DISTANCE**	5.5 miles (8.8km)
➤ **MINIMUM TIME**	2hrs 15min
➤ **ASCENT/GRADIENT**	98ft (30m)
➤ **LEVEL OF DIFFICULTY**	
➤ **PATHS**	Town pavements, meadows, railway embankment and steps
➤ **LANDSCAPE**	Water-meadows, lovely old town and disused railway
➤ **SUGGESTED MAPS**	OS Explorer 237 Norwich
➤ **START/FINISH**	Grid reference: TG 109014
➤ **DOG FRIENDLINESS**	Dogs must be kept on lead in reserves
➤ **PARKING**	Pay-and-display car park off Market Street in Wymondham
➤ **PUBLIC TOILETS**	At car park

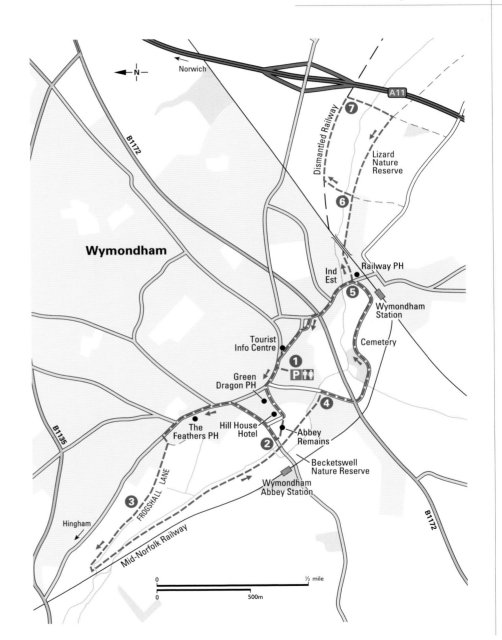

*Enjoy the countryside
and the churches around
an ancient market town.*

Reepham and Salle

*ABOVE: The interior of St Peter and St Paul
church at Salle, can be dated by the arms of
Henry V above the doorway (1405-20)
LEFT: An exterior view of St Peter and
St Paul church at Salle*

R eepham has one churchyard, but three churches once graced its confines. Two of these still exist, sitting oddly side by side right in the centre of this pretty Norfolk market town. The biggest is St Michael's, dominating the Market Place with its tall tower. It is used as a hall rather than a place of worship and has suffered from over-enthusiastic restoration. Next to it is St Mary's, which was also ravaged by the Victorians. Parts date from the 13th century, and there is a handsome effigy of a reclining Sir Roger de Kerdiston (died 1337), and his son William. All that remains of All Saints', the third church, is a wall that survived the demolition of the rest of the building in 1796.

A Trilogy of Churches

There is a reason why Reepham ended up with three churches in one yard, although it's not obvious. Reepham was originally more than one parish and in William I's Domesday Book it was closely associated with the settlements at Kerdiston, Whitwell and Hackford. All Saints' belonged to Hackford, St Michael's to Whitwell, and St Mary's to Reepham and Kerdiston. This curious set-up seems to have worked remarkably well. In 1543, Hackford's church became ruinous, probably after a fire, and the parishioners moved to share with Whitwell. Eventually, the parishes lost their separate identities and merged into Reepham.

Reepham's Rise and Fall

In the 19th century, the town was prosperous, with its brickworks, horse-training centre, a pair of tanneries and a brewery. It had a Wednesday market and a stock fair, and was served by two fire engines and a company of the Third Norfolk Rifle Volunteers. Railway stations opened in Reepham and Whitwell in 1882, built by men with colourful names like Lumpy Ling, Spitting Joe and Sam Shirt. Unusually, the railway did not bring greater prosperity to Reepham, but served to secure its demise. Cheaper goods became available from outside and local industries began to lose customers. By the end of the century, the population had dropped from 1,800 to 400.

There are still many treasures to discover in Reepham. The Old Brewery House, now a hotel, was built in the early 1700s, and the King's Arms is a former coaching inn dating from the 17th century. There was once a windmill situated on Ollands Road, but the local people objected to it so much that they planted fast-growing trees near by to prevent the wind from turning its sails. The devious ploy seemed to have worked and the miller was forced to move to a more reliable spot on the Norwich Road.

walk directions

1 From the car park turn right towards the Methodist church and turn left up Kerdiston Road, signposted 'Byway to Guestwick'. At the junction with Smuggler's Lane, take the path left into the CaSu Park. Take the footpath ahead of you, then bear to the right each time paths meet, and you will emerge through trees on to the lane again. Turn left and walk under a bridge.

2 Continue along the road to Manor Farm, then keep straight on to a track. At first the track is gravelled, then changes to grass. Watch out for the point near the end of the field where the path takes a dive to the left through the trees. The path then emerges on to a wide track.

3 Turn right along the track and take the next turning to your right, with the splendid tower of Salle church ahead. Stay on the track, looking for the occasional circular walk markers. When the track ends at a lane, turn left and continue to the next junction.

4 At the junction, turn right by Gatehouse Farm and walk up Salle's High Street to the church. There is a bench in the gate for the weary to rest. On leaving the church, cross the road and walk behind the two buildings opposite the church to the far left-hand corner of the village green, and turn right on to a wide green path. Walk along the edge of a field with fir trees on your right, ignoring the footpath to your left, until you reach the end of the plantation.

5 Turn right towards the road and then left along the side of a hedge. Continue until the path emerges on to a lane and turn left until you reach a junction.

6 At the junction, take the path that leads under the old railway bridge on to Marriott's Way. Walk along this cycle route past Reepham Station, complete with its platform. Continue until the path crosses a road, and you see some steps to your right. Walk down them, cross a stile, and turn right under the bridge. Walk along this lane to reach a fork, where you bear right to the car park.

walk information

➤ **DISTANCE**	5.25 miles (8.4km)
➤ **MINIMUM TIME**	2hrs 30min
➤ **ASCENT/GRADIENT**	82ft (25m)
➤ **LEVEL OF DIFFICULTY**	
➤ **PATHS**	Field paths and trackways; beware poor signposting, 3 stiles
➤ **LANDSCAPE**	Lively market town, peaceful village and rural Norfolk
➤ **SUGGESTED MAPS**	OS Explorer 238 Dereham & Aylsham
➤ **START/FINISH**	Grid reference: TG 099229
➤ **DOG FRIENDLINESS**	Can run free, but must be on lead on bridleway to Salle
➤ **PARKING**	Free town car park on Station Road, Reepham
➤ **PUBLIC TOILETS**	Town centre, clearly signposted; also in Reepham Station

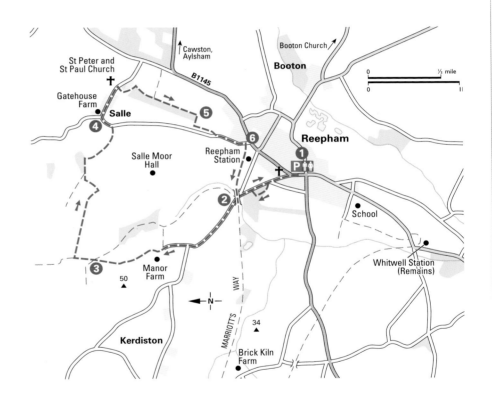

Enjoy some of the loveliest scenery in Norfolk as you stroll through the grounds of Blickling Hall.

The Weavers' Way to Blickling

For the walker, Blickling Hall is probably the best of the many National Trust properties found in Norfolk. The River Bure meanders pleasantly to the north of its grounds, which are full of shady mature trees, there is a quiet lake to stroll around and the grounds are full of fascinating buildings and monuments.

ABOVE: A row of houses, cottages and shops in the nearby Aylsham High Street
LEFT: Blickling Hall was modified extensively between 1618 and 1629

A Chequered History

The ancient manor of Blickling once belonged to King Harold who built the first house here. He was defeated at Hastings by William the Conqueror in 1066, who seized Blickling for himself, then passed it to a man who later became Bishop of Thetford. The manor remained in the hands of successive bishops until it passed to a line of soldiers. One of these, Nicholas Dagworth, built a moated house here in the 1390s. Eventually, Blickling came into the possession of Sir John Fastolf, widely believed to be the inspiration for Shakespeare's Falstaff, and then passed to the Boleyn family, where it remained until Anne Boleyn's execution by Henry VIII. The Boleyns lost a good deal of property after Anne's dramatic fall from grace and Blickling eventually came into the hands of the Hobart family in 1616.

The Hobarts made drastic changes, almost completely rebuilding the house between 1618 and 1629. Instead of following the contemporary craze for new Classical architecture, the Hobarts remained firmly traditional, and as a result the house is one of the finest examples of Jacobean architecture in the country. It was designed by Robert Lyminge, who also built Hatfield House in Essex. The building is made of brick with stone dressings, and has a pair of handsome corner towers.

From Russia With Love

Blickling is a veritable treasure house. Perhaps its most famous acquisition is the magnificent tapestry that hangs in the Peter-the-Great Room. This belonged to John Hobart, who was described by Horace Walpole as painfully transparent. He therefore appears an odd choice to appoint as Ambassador to Catherine of Russia, but to Russia he went and he seems to have made a success of his posting. It was during this sojourn that he bought the remarkable tapestry depicting the Tsar prancing along on his horse with the carnage of Poltava in the background.

The park has its origins in the 18th century and was once much bigger, before financial considerations forced its owners to sell off parcels of it. There was already a lake on the land, but the Hobarts had it enlarged in 1762. They built themselves a racecourse in 1773. It still stands on the Aylsham Road and is known as the Tower House (privately owned). Enjoy the lake and the 4,777 acres (1,935ha) of beautiful woods and gardens, as this walk takes you on a pleasant amble up to the north of the hall.

walk directions

1 Go towards the National Trust visitor centre and take the gravel path to its left, past the Buckinghamshire Arms. At the drive, turn left signed to the park and lake. Keep right and go through gates into Blickling Park. Keep ahead at a fork and follow the Weavers' Way, eventually to go through a gate into The Beeches. Continue ahead at a crossing of paths along the right-hand field-edge. On nearing a house, follow the path right, then left to a lane.

2 Turn left at the lane, following its winding path until you pass Mill Cottage, complete with mill pond, on your right and Mill Farm on your left. The mixed deciduous Great Wood on your left belongs to the National Trust. Leave the woods and walk through the pretty Bure Valley for about 700yds (640m) until you see a footpath on your left (although the sign is on the right).

3 Turn left down this overgrown track, with hedgerows to the right and trees to the left. Go up a slope to Bunker's Hill Plantation (also protected by the National Trust), skirting around the edge of this before the footpath merges with a farm track. It eventually comes out on to a road.

4 Turn left and then right, on to New Road, which is signposted for Cawston and Oulton Street. This wide lane runs as straight as an arrow for about 0.75 mile (1.2km), before reaching a crossroads at the village sign for Oulton Street.

5 Turn left by the RAF memorial and its bench. The lane starts off wide, but soon narrows to a peaceful rural track. Continue along this for 1.5 miles (2.4km), passing through the thin line of trees known as the Oulton Belt and eventually arriving at Abel Heath, a small conservation area owned by the National Trust.

walk information

➤ **DISTANCE**	6.5 miles (10.4km)
➤ **MINIMUM TIME**	3hrs
➤ **ASCENT/GRADIENT**	98ft (30m)
➤ **LEVEL OF DIFFICULTY**	
➤ **PATHS**	Paved lanes and some footpaths
➤ **LANDSCAPE**	Stately house grounds and pretty agricultural land
➤ **SUGGESTED MAPS**	OS Explorer 252 Norfolk Coast East
➤ **START/FINISH**	Grid reference: TG 176285
➤ **DOG FRIENDLINESS**	Dogs must be on lead in grounds of hall
➤ **PARKING**	Blickling Hall car park on Aylsham Road (free for NT members)
➤ **PUBLIC TOILETS**	Visitor centre at Blickling Hall; also in Aylsham town centre

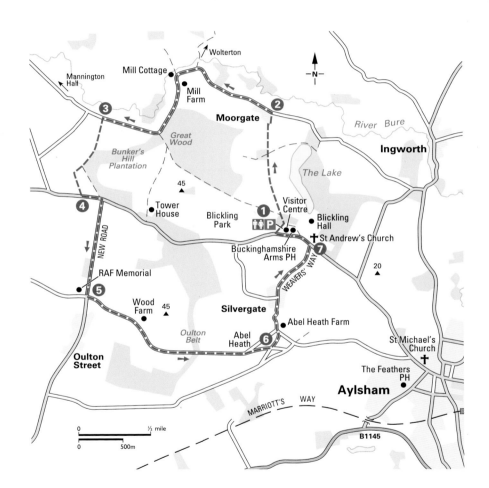

6 Turn left by the oak tree, then left at the T-junction towards Abel Heath Farm. The lane winds downhill until you reach the red-brick cottages of the little hamlet of Silvergate. You are now on the Weavers' Way long distance footpath. Pass a cemetery on your right and continue until you see St Andrew's Church (partly 14th century, but mostly Victorian). Continue on until you reach the main road.

7 Turn left, passing the Buckinghamshire Arms and the pretty 18th- and 19th-century estate cottages at the park gates on your right. Continue walking until you see signs for the car park, where you turn right.

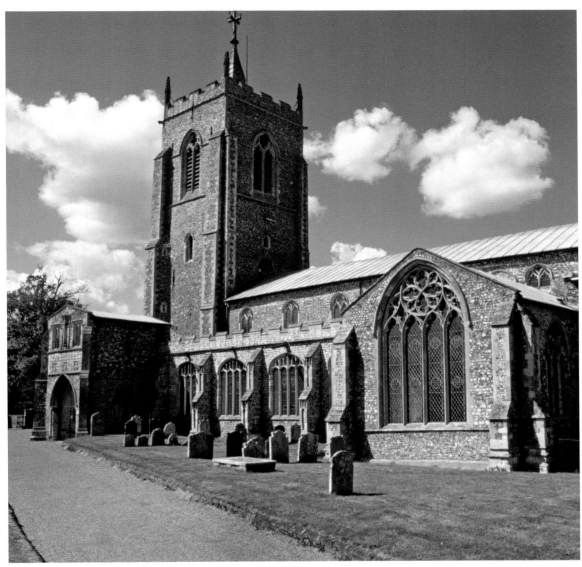

ABOVE: *The medieval church of St Michael's, Aylsham*

LEFT: *Blickling Hall and gardens*

Tread in the footsteps of wealthy medieval weavers as you explore ancient sheep-rearing country.

Worstead's Light and Durable Worsted

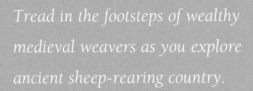

Edward III was blessed with a faithful and loyal wife, who bore him 12 children and exerted a moderating influence on his fiery Plantagent temper. Her name was Philippa of Hainault and she was the daughter of William, Count of Hainault and Zeeland. Her Flemish background made her something of an expert on the weaving trade, and it was because of Philippa that so many experienced weavers settled in Norfolk and Suffolk.

ABOVE: Worstead Railway Station
on the Bittern Line
LEFT: Worstead village centre, featuring
the Church of St Mary

A Marriage Made in Heaven

As far as medieval marriages went, Edward and Philippa's was made in heaven. He was not faithful and she was not beautiful, but they maintained a close attachment throughout their long liaison. Their children included the Black Prince, who died just two years before his long-lived father without ever taking the throne, and the intelligent, powerful John of Gaunt, who was easily one of the richest men in the world in his lifetime. All the King's children remained on surprisingly good terms with each other and the King himself, something largely attributed to Philippa's gentle nature.

Flemish Weavers

As soon as she had settled in England, Philippa realised that it did not make economic sense for vast quantities of fine wool to be produced in East Anglia for export to Flanders, where weavers made it into cloth and sold it back to the English at inflated prices. She encouraged Flemish weavers to settle in England, so they could train Englishmen in cloth production. Worstead was one of several villages that profited from their expertise.

The so-called 'Worstead villages' included North Walsham, Scottow, Tunstead and Aylsham, as well as Worstead, but it was Worstead that gave its name to the light, relatively inexpensive cloth that made these places far richer than their neighbours. By the end of the 14th century it was not the weavers of Ypres and Ghent who were setting world standards in cloth excellence, but those of Norfolk and Suffolk with their worsteds. John Paston, one of the letter-writing Norfolk Paston family, wrote in 1465 that 'I would make my doublet all worsted, for worship of Norfolk.'

Magnificent Church

In 1379 the weavers' guild was so wealthy and powerful that its members pooled their resources and built the St Mary's Church, declaring that the original St Andrew's Church was neither large nor grand enough for their village. The result is one of the loveliest parish churches in the county, with a tower that is 109ft (33m) tall, and the church itself 130ft (40m) long – astonishing proportions for a village church. Weaving in Worstead continued until the late 19th century and is practised on a much smaller scale today by some locals.

walk directions

1 From Church Plain, in the centre of Worstead, turn right into Front Street with handsome 14th-century St Mary's Church behind you and the New Inn on your right. Bend to the left, then immediately right and continue walking out of the village. The road veers to the left, then to the right. The mixed deciduous plantation to your left is called the Worstead Belt because of its long, thin shape. Pass Worstead Hall Farm (originally 16th century) on your right before plunging into shady woodland.

2 Turn left on the road signposted to Dilham. Ignore the two lanes off to the right, but follow the road round to the left when it bends sharply through woods and up a hill. Where the road turns sharp right, turn left on to the concrete lane and continue ahead until you reach a sign, stating 'Private Road'.

3 Turn right and walk along the wide track (marked as a public footpath) that leads in a straight line through a tunnel of mixed woodland. This is Carman's Lane, and it emerges on to a quiet country lane after about 0.5 mile (800m). Cross the lane, heading for the footpath opposite. There is a hedge right in front of you, with fields on either side, and a footpath sign. Keep to the left of the hedge and walk along the edge of the field until you see signs for another footpath off to your left.

4 Turn left along this path, walking until the red roofs of Dairyhouse Barn come into view. Just after this, there is a T-junction of footpaths. Take the one to the right, a farm track called Green Lane, and walk along it until you reach a paved road.

5 Go left, along a lane that is bordered by tall hedgerows which are filled with nesting birds in the spring. You pass a few neat houses on your left before the lane ends in a T-junction.

6 Turn right opposite Rose Cottage and Windy Ridge on to Honing Row, and walk for a few paces until you reach Geoffrey the Dyer's House on your right. This dates from the 16th century, and has unusually tall ceilings in order to accommodate the merchant's looms. The site of the old manor house lies up this lane, too.

7 Turn left opposite Geoffrey's house to return to your park place and the start of the walk.

walk information

➤ DISTANCE	4 miles (6.4km)
➤ MINIMUM TIME	1hr 45min
➤ ASCENT/GRADIENT	33ft (10m)
➤ LEVEL OF DIFFICULTY	
➤ PATHS	Easy public footpaths and some paved country lanes
➤ LANDSCAPE	Woodland and agricultural land
➤ SUGGESTED MAPS	OS Explorer OL40 The Broads
➤ START/FINISH	Grid reference: TG 302260
➤ DOG FRIENDLINESS	Dogs can run free
➤ PARKING	On Church Plain
➤ PUBLIC TOILETS	In pub car park (follow signposts)

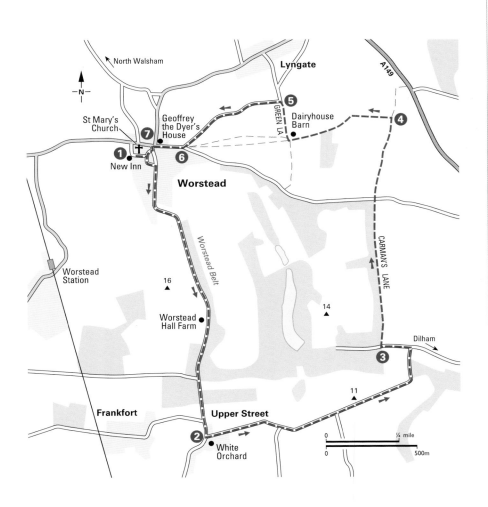

Explore the countryside around
a Roman fortress and walk in
the footsteps of Queen Boudica.

A Revolting Queen at Caistor St Edmund

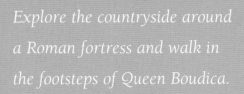

When the Romans invaded Britain, they built arrow-straight roads, established well-run, prosperous towns and developed industries like tile-making, salt and potteries, the likes of which had not been seen before. But not all the local tribes were pleased to be a part of the Roman Empire.

ABOVE: A country lane near
Caistor St Edmund
LEFT: The nave at the Church of St
Edmund dates from 1050 AD

Rebel Queen

One such rebel against the Romans was Boudica, who had been married to King Prasutagus of the Iceni. The trouble started when Prasutagus died in AD 60. He was barely cold in his grave before the Roman procurator's men arrived to grab property and money, and troops appeared to impose military law. One Roman insulted Boudica, who responded with anger, and in retaliation was flogged and her daughters raped. News of this outrage spread like wildfire throughout East Anglia and the revolt was born. Her headquarters are said to have been at or near Venta Icenorum at Caistor.

Contemporary accounts tell us that Boudica was tall, with fierce eyes and a strident voice. She had a mane of tawny hair that tumbled to her waist and she wore a striking multicoloured tunic, a gold neck torc and a cloak held by a brooch. Female rulers were not unknown to the Iceni and they quickly rallied to her fiery speeches of rebellion and revenge. Other tribes joined the throng as Boudica's army moved against the Romans, carrying huge shields and wearing their best battle gear.

Retaliation

From Venta Icenorum to Colchester they marched, probably using the recently completed Roman road. The army grew until it was 100,000 strong, all angry and determined to exact revenge on their hated oppressors. Meanwhile, Colchester was wholly unprepared for the attack, because the civilians had been assured there was nothing to worry about – they had well-trained Roman soldiers to defend them. But as soon as the garrison spotted the enormous, vengeful throng, they abandoned their posts and fled for safety inside the temple of Claudius. The civilians were left to fend for themselves. A massacre followed of the most shocking magnitude. No one was spared and as many as 20,000 were killed. The wooden town was burned to the ground and the stone temple fell two days later. Boudica then moved on to London and St Albans, where the bloodshed continued.

The Roman general Suetonius marched to meet her and the two forces met near St Albans. Suetonius' well-trained military machine was outnumbered by the Britons, but reports say that the Romans destroyed 80,000 of the larger force – an appalling number of dead for any battle. Boudica probably poisoned herself after the defeat, but her legend lives on. This walk takes you through the lands she once ruled, some of it along the 38-mile (61km) footpath named in her honour.

1 The first part of the walk follows the marked circular trail around Venta Icenorum, so go through the gate next to the notice board at the car park. The trail is marked by red and white circles. Climb a flight of steps, then go down six to reach the huge bank that protected the town, with a deep ditch to your left. Now head west, towards the River Tas.

2 Turn right by the bench, past fragments of old walls, then right again when you reach a longer section of wall, still following the trail markers. Go through a gate, then walk along the side of the bank with more wall to your right. Go up the steps, then descend again to the ditch on the eastern edge of the town. Go past St Edmund's Church and when you reach the car park, go through it. Cross the road, then go through the gate opposite then turn right. You are now on Boudica's Way.

3 Just after the brick cottages take the tiny unmarked lane to your left, still following Boudica's Way. Go up a hill, keep straight at the next junction and keep walking until you see Whiteford Hall.

4 Turn left up Valley Farm Lane, following the yellow Boudica's Way markers. After the farm, look for the footpath sign to your right. Take this and keep to your right, along the side of a hedge. Jig right, then immediately left and keep walking until you reach a paved lane. Turn left and then look for another footpath sign, which you'll find to your right.

5 Take the footpath, and follow the markers down a hill and up the other side. It's important to keep to the footpaths here, because there are plenty of signs indicating private property. At the top of the field, take the left-hand path through the woods, continuing to follow the yellow markers for Boudica's Way.

6 At a four-way junction, go right across a field, still on Boudica's Way. Continue around a chalk quarry until you see a gate to the right. Follow the path straight across the field. Turn left on to Arminghall Lane.

7 At the T-junction, go left using the gravel path and the verges. Descend a hill into the village of Caistor St Edmund, and follow signs for the Roman town, passing 17th-century Caistor Hall to your left. Keep walking until you reach the signs for Venta Icenorum, then turn right into the car park.

walk information

➤ DISTANCE	6.25 miles (10.1km)
➤ MINIMUM TIME	3hrs
➤ ASCENT/GRADIENT	279ft (85m) ▲▲▲
➤ LEVEL OF DIFFICULTY	🚶🚶🚶
➤ PATHS	Paved road and public footpaths, several sets of steps
➤ LANDSCAPE	Rolling farmland and an archaeological site
➤ SUGGESTED MAPS	OS Explorer 237 Norwich
➤ START/FINISH	Grid reference: TG 232032
➤ DOG FRIENDLINESS	Dogs must be on lead in Roman town
➤ PARKING	South Norfolk Council and Norfolk Archaeological Trust car park at Roman fort (free)
➤ PUBLIC TOILETS	None on route

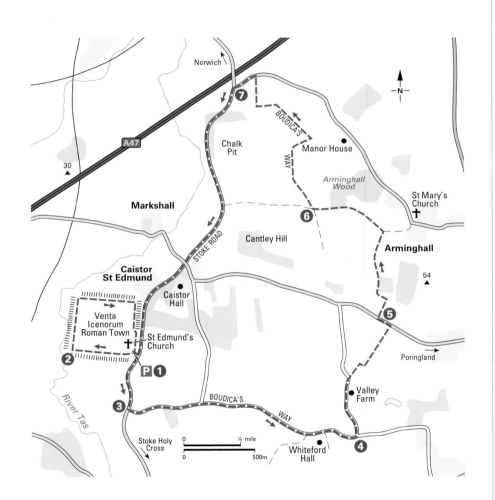

From the coast at Overstrand through the Poppylands area, beloved by the Victorians.

Overstrand to Northrepps

ABOVE: *Overstrand's village sign*
LEFT: *The pebbly beach at Cromer*

There is a constant battle raging between the sea and the land at Overstrand, and although the land is holding its own thanks to some serious sea defences, it looks as though the water will be the eventual winner. The cliffs around Overstrand are crumbling slowly and are being reclaimed by the North Sea. Further east, the cliffs are so precarious that there is no access to them until you reach Mundesley. In the 14th century, the sea swept away the land on which the Church of St Martin stood, and the villagers were obliged to build another – the one you can see today.

Poppylands

This walk has more to offer than eroded cliffs and tales of disappearing churches. It wanders through Poppylands, the name given to the area by poet Clement William Scott in late-Victorian times. Scott loved this part of Norfolk and wrote a series of newspaper articles about the unspoiled beauty of its fishing villages, rolling farmland and rugged coastline. His descriptions were so vivid that visitors flocked to the area and the humble fishing village developed to accommodate the rich and famous.

A Popular Place

Houses were designed by famous architects like Edwin Lutyens and Arthur William Bloomfield. The Pleasaunce was designed by Lutyens with gardens by Gertrude Jekyll for Gladstone's Chief Whip, Lord Battersea, and splendid Overstrand Hall was built for the banker Lord Hillingdon in 1899. Even the Churchill family had a residence here.

As the population grew to include an upper-class community, more facilities were needed to accommodate them. St Martin's Church had become unsafe in the 18th century and Christ Church was raised in 1867 to replace it. But the newcomers preferred the ancient simplicity of St Martin's and so it was rebuilt and restored in 1911–14. For those who preferred nonconformist worship, there was a handsome Methodist chapel, designed in 1898 by Lutyens. It is an odd building, with a brick lower floor and arched clerestory windows in the upper floor.

After strolling through the farmland south of Overstrand, you reach the village of Northrepps, which became famous when Verily Anderson wrote a book called *The Northrepps Grandchildren*, describing what life was like at Northrepps Hall.

RIGHT: Fishing boats on the beach at Cromer

walk directions

1 Go right, out of the car park on to Paul's Lane. Pass the Old Rectory, then walk along the pavement on the left. Pass Arden Close, then look for the public footpath sign on your left. Follow this alley until you reach a road.

2 Cross the road, aiming for the sign 'Private Drive Please Drive Slowly'. To the left is a footpath. Go up this track, then take the path to the left of the gate to Stanton Farm. Climb a hill, taking the path to the right when the main track bears left. At the brow follow the path towards a line of trees. Go downhill, eventually reaching Toll Cottage.

3 Take the lane ahead, passing Broadgate Close. At the Northrepps village sign and a T-junction, turn left on to Church Street, keeping left. Pass the Foundry Arms and look for the phone box and bus stop, beyond which lies Craft Lane.

4 Turn right along Craft Lane, using the pavement until a sign marks this as a 'quiet lane' for walkers. After 700yds (640m) there is a Paston Way sign on your left. Take this through the woods, and bear left when it becomes a track to Hungry Hill farm.

5 At the lane next to the farm, turn left. After a few paces go right, following 'Circular Walk Paston Way' signs. Follow this gravel track towards the radar scanner installation.

6 Keep left where the track bends towards the radar tower, following the footpath signs. The path descends through woods, passing under a disused railway bridge before meeting the main road. Cross this, then turn left to walk on the pavement for a few paces before turning right along Coast Road. When the road starts to bends, look out for signs to Overstrand Promenade.

7 Go down the steep ramp to your right to arrive at a concrete walkway. Up to your left you will see the remains of fallen houses in the crumbling cliffs. Follow the walkway (or you can walk on the sand, if you prefer) until you reach a slipway for boats. To the left of the slipway you'll find a zig-zag pathway.

8 Follow this upwards to the top of the cliffs. The car park is just ahead of you.

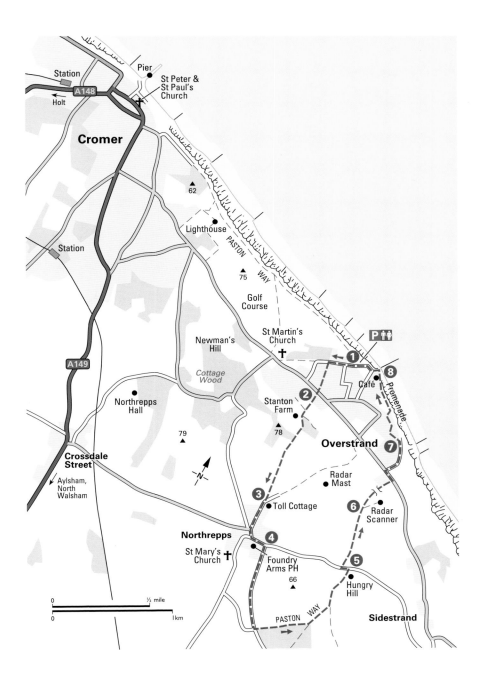

walk information

DISTANCE	4 miles (6.4km)
MINIMUM TIME	2hrs
ASCENT/GRADIENT	295ft (90m)
LEVEL OF DIFFICULTY	
PATHS	Farm tracks, footpaths, quiet lanes
LANDSCAPE	Attractive rolling farmland
SUGGESTED MAPS	OS Explorer 252 Norfolk Coast East
START/FINISH	Grid reference: TG 247410
DOG FRIENDLINESS	Dogs not allowed on Promenade
PARKING	Pay-and-display car park on Coast Road in Overstrand
PUBLIC TOILETS	At car park

93

*Enjoy the windmill-studded skyline
in this lovely stroll to the River Ant.*

Ludham and the Broads

No visit to Norfolk would be complete without a trip to the Broads National Park. This is a patchwork of interlinked streams, lakes and channels that wind sluggishly over the flat land to the east of Norwich. Three major rivers – the Bure, Waveney and Yare – supply most of the water to the meres, ponds and marshes before entering the great tidal basin at Breydon Water and flowing into the sea at Great Yarmouth.

ABOVE: *A carved and colourfully painted sign welcomes people to the town of Ludham*
RIGHT: *The waters of the River Ant at How Hill in the Norfolk Broads*

A Brief History of the Broads

Despite the fact that the Broads comprise one of England's best wilderness areas, most natural historians and archaeologists accept that their origin lies in ancient human activity. They were formed when local people mined the extensive peat deposits here, cutting away the fuel to form neat vertical sides. An obvious question for any visitor is how did these ancient folk, with their primitive tools, carve out these huge areas before they filled up? The answer lies in the fact that the sea level was lower in the past and none of the Broads are very deep, mostly less than 15ft (5m), suggesting the peat was cut until it became too boggy.

So, when did all this happen? No one really knows, since maps of the area are lacking until about 400 years ago. Fritton and the linked Ormesby–Rollesby–Filby broads appear on a map of 1574, and Domesday records indicate that there was demand for peat from Norwich and Great Yarmouth. Documents written in the 13th and 14th centuries tell of devastating floods and mention that turf production around South Walsham declined dramatically. Perhaps it was then that the miners abandoned their workings and left the area to become a paradise for native birds and plants.

New industries sprang up, using sedge and reed for thatching and alder wood for brush making. These small-scale projects kept the waterways open. Their decline since the First World War has meant that open fenland has gradually become dense alder carr (wet woodland dominated by alder). Ancient waterways, that once saw traditional Norfolk wherries (sailing craft) transporting goods, are silting up and the heavy use of fertilisers on arable land causes algal blooms. You will see what the Broads Authority is doing about these problems when you visit the How Hill nature reserve.

RIGHT: A sailboat navigates Hickling Broad

walk directions

1 Leave the car park and the busy marina and walk up Horsefen Road, going the same way that you came in to park.

2 Turn left at the end of Horsefen Road, walking along the footpath that runs inside a hedge next to the road. When you see the King's Arms ahead, turn right up the road towards 'Catfield'. After a few paces turn left on to School Road. Houses soon give way to countryside. Take the permissive path on the right of a hedge next to the road. Go straight across the next junction, following the sign for How Hill.

3 Turn right along a lane signposted 'How Hill'. The lane winds and twists, and is fairly narrow, which makes for pleasant walking. You will soon reach How Hill House, a sail-less windmill and How Hill nature reserve. There are marked trails through the reserve, if you feel like a pleasant diversion. When you have finished, continue down How Hill Road. Pass Grove Farm Gallery and Studio on your right, and look for a red-brick barn followed by a lane, also on your right.

4 Turn right down Wateringpiece Lane. Pass the modern water tower on your left and walk past some fields. Look for the public footpath crossing the road. Go left along the bridleway that runs along the edge of a field until it ends at a lane.

LEFT: A River Ant Nature Conservancy Cottage at How Hill

5 Turn right on Catfield Road and walk along the verge on the right, where there is a footpath. This road can be busy in the summer, when thousands of visitors flock to Ludham and How Hill. Ignore the lane on your left, heading to Potter Heigham, and continue walking ahead until you reach a crossroads by Ludham Methodist Church.

6 Go straight across, walking a few paces until you reach the next junction with Ludham church ahead of you. Turn left along Yarmouth, Road, then right into Horsefen Road. This will take you back to the car park.

walk information

➤ **DISTANCE**	5 miles (8km)
➤ **MINIMUM TIME**	2hrs
➤ **ASCENT/GRADIENT**	33ft (10m)
➤ **LEVEL OF DIFFICULTY**	
➤ **PATHS**	Quiet country lanes and grassy footpaths
➤ **LANDSCAPE**	Reed-fringed broad and gently rolling agricultural land
➤ **SUGGESTED MAPS**	OS Explorer OL40 The Broads
➤ **START/FINISH**	Grid reference: TG 391180
➤ **DOG FRIENDLINESS**	Not permitted in nature reserve, on lead through farmland
➤ **PARKING**	Womack Staithe in Horsefen Road, Ludham
➤ **PUBLIC TOILETS**	At Womack Staithe

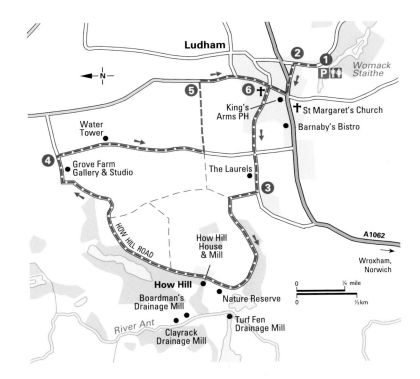

Explore whispering reed beds and silent windmills and finish at pub owned by the National Trust.

Around the Mysterious Horsey Mere

ABOVE: Horsey Church dates from the 11th century
LEFT: The River Thurne and the restored Horsey Drainage Mill

In 1938, a devastating combination of high tides and storms occurred around Horsey. The sea surged inland, flooding buildings and fields, and forcing people to evacuate their homes. It was four months before the water subsided and the villagers were able to resume normal life, although it took another five years before the damaging effects of salt water on the fields was finally overcome. Horsey is barely 3ft (1m) above sea level and, as you walk around the reed-fringed mere and stroll along its many drainage channels, you will appreciate its vulnerability at the hands of the sea.

Listing Brograve Mill

Not for nothing was this area known as 'Devil's Country' in local legends. You will see part of the devil's handiwork when you pass Brograve Mill, between Horsey and Waxam. The story goes that one Thomas Brograve was determined to reclaim part of this wilderness for farming, and built a mill. The devil was furious and tried to blow it down. He did not succeed, but you will see a distinct list to the mill today, indicating that the battle was a close-run thing! Horsey has its own legend: it is said that on 13 June each year, the wailing voices of drowned children can be heard from the mere.

The village and surrounding area is now in the care of the National Trust, so its picturesque tranquillity is unlikely to be spoiled. All Saints' Church dates from the 13th century, and has an attractive thatched nave. Go inside and look for the stained-glass window in the south chancel commemorating Catherine Ursula Rising, who died in 1890. She is shown painting in her drawing room at Horsey Hall. The hall is to the south, built in 1845 for the Risings, who bought the manor from the Brograves.

Horsey Drainage Mill

The village's most famous feature is the Horsey Drainage Mill, built to pump water from the surrounding farmland. It dates from the middle of the 19th century, but was rebuilt in 1897 and again in 1912. It has four storeys of brick and a handsome weather-boarded cap in the shape of a boat. It was working in 1940 when it was struck by lightning, and was restored in 1961. Today it is owned by the National Trust and is open to visitors.

Away to the south-west is Horsey Mere, a part of the Broads and a beautiful stretch of the walk. The mere is surrounded by reed beds, which are used for thatching many of Horsey's pretty houses. This peaceful stretch of water offers a haven for countless birds, particularly in winter, when it is filled by thousands of waterfowl.

1 From the National Trust car park walk towards the toilets and take the footpath to the right of them. This leads to a footbridge. After crossing the bridge turn immediately right and follow the path along the side of Horsey Mere through reeds and alder copses. Cross a wooden bridge across a dyke and through a gate to enter a grassy water-meadow. Look for the white disc across the field. Go through a second gate and over a bridge.

2 Turn right when the path meets a brown-watered dyke (Waxham New Cut). Eventually, you will see derelict Brograve Drainage Mill ahead. Herons and other birds often perch on its battered sails, so it's worth stopping to look.

3 Turn right immediately adjacent to the mill and walk along the edge of a field. Reed beds give way to water-meadow. Cross another plank bridge and continue straight ahead. The path bends left, then right, then crosses a small lane and continues through the field opposite. At the end of the field, make a sharp left, eventually coming to another lane.

4 Go right at the lane, bearing right where it meets a track, and walk past Poppylands Café. When you reach a junction turn left, following the sign for the Nelson Head. Pass the pub on your left-hand side, then look for a well-defined footpath going off to your right.

5 Walk past the gate and continue along the wide sward ahead, with a narrow dyke on either side. When the sward divides, bear left and head for a stile at the end of the footpath. Climb this and immediately turn right to walk along a spacious field. This area is used for grazing breeding stock and you should look for signs warning about the presence of bulls. Since this part of the walk is permissive, and not a public footpath, the National Trust is within its rights to put bulls here, so it is important to check for warning signs before you venture forth. These are always prominently displayed. If this is the case, you will

have to walk back to the lane and turn left. This will take you back to the car park at the start of the walk.

6 Assuming there are no bulls to hinder your progress, climb the stile, between the field and the road, and then cross the road. The car park where the walk began is ahead of you and slightly to your right. This is a good time to explore the delights of restored Horsey Drainage Mill, which you will find just to your left.

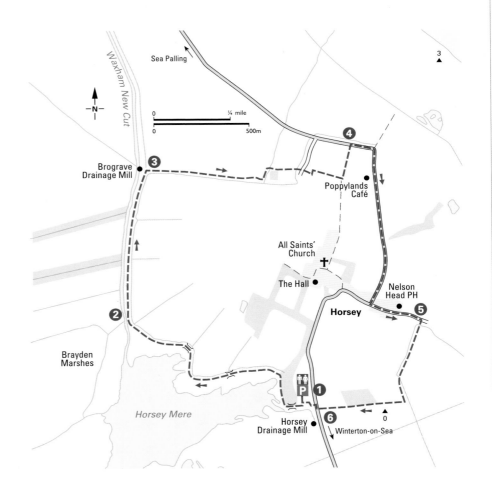

walk information

➤ **DISTANCE**	3.5 miles (5.7km)
➤ **MINIMUM TIME**	1hr 30min
➤ **ASCENT/GRADIENT**	Negligible
➤ **LEVEL OF DIFFICULTY**	
➤ **PATHS**	Marked trails along dykes (walk quietly to avoid disturbing nesting birds), 5 stiles
➤ **LANDSCAPE**	Reed-fringed drainage channels, marshy lake and water-meadows
➤ **SUGGESTED MAPS**	OS Explorer OL40 The Broads
➤ **START/FINISH**	Grid reference: TG 456223
➤ **DOG FRIENDLINESS**	On lead over farmland (livestock breeding area), avoid areas used by nesting water birds
➤ **PARKING**	National Trust pay-and-display at Horsey Drainage Mill
➤ **PUBLIC TOILETS**	At car park

ABOVE: The sun sets on the boats moored at Horsey

ABOVE: Wind-blown sand dunes and wooden groynes on a deserted sandy beach at Horsey

Vast skylines and endless reed-choked marshes make you feel very small in this fascinating landscape.

Breydon Water and Burgh Castle

ABOVE: *A grey and overcast day on Breydon water*
LEFT: *A poppy field in front of the Norman Church of St Peter and St Paul, Burgh Castle*

Near the western reaches of Breydon Water there is a Roman fort, a wind pump owned by the National Trust and an atmospheric pub, which is inaccessible to cars. However, there is an obstacle preventing you from wandering to and from these sites: the River Yare. At the start of the walk you will see the river begin to widen, until it forms the vast, silt-slippery flats of Breydon Water that lies between the Roman castle and the mill and pub, so the only way to see all three on foot is to walk around it!

Mysterious Waters

This part of the Broads is perhaps the most mysterious and lonely of all, and the fact that few roads cross the marshes that radiate out from Breydon Water means that it is generally people-free. This suits birds very nicely, and the Royal Society for the Protection of Birds (RSPB) manages quite a large part of it, maintaining it as a nature reserve to encourage both rare and common species. Halvergate Marshes, to the west, is an alluvial basin that is home to shoveller, snipe, lapwing, yellow wagtails and redshank.

Berney Arms Mill

Berney Arms Mill is one of the most spectacular mills in the country. It is in perfect working order and stands some 70ft (21m) high, making it the tallest marsh mill in Norfolk or Suffolk. It was built in 1870 and now houses a small museum. Downstream is the Berney Arms, accessible only to people who walk or navigate the silty channels in their boats.

An Impressive Fortress

Gariannonum, or Burgh Castle, lies on the opposite shore of the river. Originally this would have commanded an imposing position looking towards Caister, but changes in the sea level and silting up have relegated it to a quiet part of the river. It was built in the 3rd century AD to defend the Roman province from marauding Saxons, and was an impressive fortress. Even today, visitors will see walls rising to more than 15ft (5m). This stronghold is said to have been the place where the Irish missionary St Fursey arrived in England in about AD 630. One of the first things he did was to found a monastery, which he called Cnobheresburg, although nothing remains of this today.

Later, Fursey removed himself to France, so that he could become a proper hermit. He founded a monastery near Paris and when he died, his body declined to rot. He was declared a saint, and various parts of his corpse toured the country until most were destroyed during the French Revolution. The head was said to have survived, though, and is still an object of reverence in Péronne in Picardy.

LEFT: The Berney Arms Mill beside the River Yare

walk directions

1 Leave the car park and walk uphill towards the church. Take the path to the left of the church, through a kissing gate, signposted to the castle. After a few steps and another kissing gate, you will see a well-trodden path cutting diagonally across the fields. Follow this until you reach the spectacularly grand walls of the Roman fort Gariannonum, aiming for the gap in the middle.

2 Go through the gap, and explore the castle, then aim for 28 steps in the far right-hand corner. Descend the steps, walk alongside a field, and look for 40 steps leading down to the river bank. Turn right along the Angles Way and continue until you reach a junction of paths behind Church Farm Hotel. This stretch of riverside and reedbeds may be flooded after heavy rain.

3 Turn left towards the double gates, which will take you on a long (3-mile/4.8km) uninterrupted trail along the edge of Breydon Water.

The path sticks closely by the river, following a raised flood bank with glorious views in all directions across the pancake-flat marshes and mudflats. Eventually, you will see the tall struts of Breydon Bridge in the distance.

4 Pass through a gate to enter the Herbert Barnes Riverside Park. When the path divides, take the right-hand fork, leaving the river and winding across a meadow to Broadland Rugby Club, where you climb to the A12.

5 If you want to avoid a busy stretch of main road, turn around at this point and retrace your steps along the river, enjoying the views of Breydon Water in the opposite direction. Otherwise, turn right on the A12, keeping carefully to the right-hand verge, and continue for just over 0.5 mile (800m) to a roundabout with a retail park on your right. Keep right on a pedestrian and cycle path beside the road. After passing the entrance signs for Bradwell and just before an industrial estate, look for a gap in the hedge and steps leading down to a footpath across the marshes on your right.

walk information

➤ **DISTANCE**	8 miles (12.9km)
➤ **MINIMUM TIME**	3hrs
➤ **ASCENT/GRADIENT**	49ft (15m)
➤ **LEVEL OF DIFFICULTY**	
➤ **PATHS**	Riverside paths, footpaths, busy stretch of road, several steps, 1 stile
➤ **LANDSCAPE**	Marshland, expanses of mudflats and some arable land
➤ **SUGGESTED MAPS**	OS Explorer OL40 The Broads
➤ **START/FINISH**	Grid reference: TG 476050
➤ **DOG FRIENDLINESS**	Must be on lead at all times along edge of Breydon Water
➤ **PARKING**	Car park near Church Farm Hotel
➤ **PUBLIC TOILETS**	None on route

6 Turn down the footpath, which takes you between the estate and the marshes. After 0.75 mile (1.2km), turn left on to a wide track for about 250yds (229m), then take a footpath through a gap in the hedge to your right, past the farm buildings of Bradwell Hall, to a crossroads.

7 Keep ahead through a rusty gate and past an abandoned house, then follow the path between the fields. Cross a stile and across the fields to a short farm track, which bends left to arrive at High Road. Turn right and right again on to Back Lane. This quiet lane bends left, passing houses and an Anglian Water station, before emerging on to High Road at the Queens Head.

8 Turn right and keep climbing until you see the church. Turn right into the car park.

LEFT: A section of stone wall at Burgh Castle

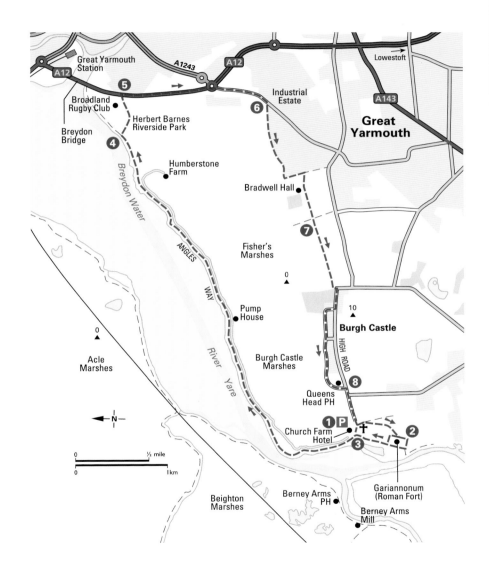

Walking in Safety

All these walks are suitable for any reasonably fit person, but less experienced walkers should try the easier walks first. Route finding is usually straightforward, but you will find that an Ordnance Survey map is a useful addition to the route maps and descriptions.

Risks

Although each walk here has been researched with a view to minimising the risks to the walkers who follow its route, no walk in the countryside can be considered to be completely free from risk. Walking in the outdoors will always require a degree of common sense and judgement to ensure that it is as safe as possible.

- Be particularly careful on cliff paths and in upland terrain, where the consequences of a slip can be very serious.
- Remember to check tidal conditions before walking on the seashore.
- Some sections of route are by, or cross, busy roads. Take care and remember traffic is a danger even on minor country lanes.
- Be careful around farmyard machinery and livestock, especially if you have children with you.
- Be aware of the consequences of changes in the weather and check the forecast before you set out. Carry spare clothing and a torch if you are walking in the winter months. Remember the weather can change very quickly at any time of the year, and in moorland and heathland areas, mist and fog can make route finding much harder. Don't set out in these conditions unless you are confident of your navigation skills in poor visibility. In summer remember to take account of the heat and sun; wear a hat and carry spare water.
- On walks away from centres of population you should carry a whistle and survival bag. If you do have an accident requiring the emergency services, make a note of your position as accurately as possible and dial 999.

Acknowledgements

The Automobile Association would like to thank the following photographers, companies and picture libraries for their assistance in the preparation of this book.

Abbreviations for the picture credits are as follows: (t) top; (b) bottom; (l) left; (r) right; (AA) AA World Travel Library.

2/3 AA/A Baker; 5 AA/T Mackie; 6 AA/T Mackie; 7bl AA/T Mackie; 7bcl AA/S&O Mathews; 7bcr AA/A Baker; 7br AA/T Mackie; 10 11/A Baker; 10/11 AA/T Mackie; 12/13 © Holmes Garden Photos/Alamy; 13 © David Wootton/Alamy; 16 AA/A Baker; 16/17 AA/T Souter; 20/21 AA/A Baker; 21 © Rick Edwards/Alamy; 22/23 AA/T Mackie; 24 © 2008 photolibrary.com; 26/27 AA/T Mackie; 27 AA/T Mackie; 30/31 AA/T Mackie; 32 AA/D Forss; 32/33 AA/D Forss; 36/37 AA/T Mackie; 37 AA/S&O Mathews; 40/41 AA/T Mackie; 42/43 AA/T Mackie; 43 AA/M Birkitt; 44/45 AA/T Mackie; 46 AA/T Souter; 48 AA/A Baker; 48/49 AA/M Birkitt; 52 AA/S&O Mathews; 52/53 AA/S&O Mathews; 56/57 AA/T Mackie; 57 AA/T Souter; 58/59 AA/T Mackie; 60 AA/T Mackie; 52/63 © E&E Image Library/Heritage-Images/Imagestate; 63 © Topfoto; 66/67 © Quentin Bargate/Alamy; 67 © Howard Taylor/Alamy; 68/69 © Nicholas Wilby/Alamy; 70 AA/S&O Mathews; 72/73 AA/M Birkitt; 73 AA/M Birkitt; 76/77 AA/T Souter; 77 AA/A Baker; 80/81 AA/S&O Mathews; 81 AA/A Baker; 82 © Andrew Crowhurst/Alamy; 83 © Jim Laws/Alamy; 86/87 © Tom Mackie/Alamy; 87 AA/A Baker; 90/91 AA/A Baker; 91 AA/A Baker; 92/93 AA/T Mackie; 94 AA/T Souter; 94/95 AA/T Souter; 96/97 AA/T Mackie; 98 AA/T Souter; 100/101 AA/T Mackie; 101 AA/M Birkitt; 104 AA/T Mackie; 105 AA/M Birkitt; 106/107 AA/A Baker; 107 AA/S&O Mathews; 108/109 AA/A Perkins; 110 AA/A Baker;

Every effort has been made to trace the copyright holders, and we apologise in advance for any accidental errors. We would be happy to apply the corrections in the following edition of this publication.